Training Your Puppy in 5 Minutes

A QUICK, EASY AND HUMANE APPROACH

A KENNEL CLUB BOOK®

AUTHOR BIOGRAPHY

The author, Miriam Fields-Babineau, with Golden Retriever puppies.

Miriam Fields-Babineau has been training dogs and other animals professionally since 1978. She has owned and operated Training Unlimited Animal Training and Animal Actors, Inc., for 25 years. She teaches people how to communicate with and train their dogs, of any age or breed, specializing in behavioral problem-solving.

Ms. Fields-Babineau has authored many animal-related books, including *Dog Training with a Head Halter* (Barron's Educational Series, Inc.), the e-book *How to Become a Professional Dog Trainer* (Intellectua.com), *Dog Training Basics* (Sterling Publishing Co., Inc.) and many more. She writes numerous articles for trade magazines, such as the award-winning *Off-Lead Magazine* and *Practical Horseman*. She has produced the videos *The First Hello*, which addresses how to prepare a dog for the arrival of an infant, and *Dog Training with a Comfort Trainer*, which demonstrates how to train a dog using her head-halter design, the Comfort Trainer.

Ms. Fields-Babineau also provides animals for television, film and advertising, having worked with *National Geographic*, Animal Planet, the History Channel, Warner Films, Orion Films, the Discovery Channel, CBS, the Family Channel and many more. When not training other people's animal companions, she travels the country, performing in equine and canine competitions as well as exhibiting the skills of her trained felines.

**Photographs by Evan Cohen,
with additional photos by**
Bernd Brinkmann, Miriam Fields-Babineau,
Isabelle Francais and Carol Ann Johnson.

The publisher would like to thank all of the owners
of the dogs featured in this book.

KENNEL CLUB BOOKS®: TRAINING YOUR PUPPY IN 5 MINUTES
ISBN: 1-59378-593-3

Copyright © 2005 Kennel Club Books, LLC
308 Main Street, Allenhurst, NJ 07711 USA
Cover Design Patented: US 6,435,559 B2 • Printed in South Korea

10 9 8 7 6 5 4 3 2 1

Training Your Puppy in 5 Minutes

A QUICK, EASY AND HUMANE APPROACH

By Miriam Fields-Babineau

Contents

Busy puppies are happy puppies. On-leash strolls in the park are good exercise, as growing pups should not have strenuous activity that stresses their developing bodies.

INTRODUCTION

Most dog owners believe that it takes many hours per day to train their puppies. They try to work with them for 20 or 30 minutes at a time, yet only receive 5 to 10 minutes of puppy attention span. With the puppy's loss of interest, the puppy owner becomes frustrated.

Many trainers will not begin working with dogs until they reach four to six months of age, or even older. They believe that puppies cannot learn anything until this time. Even many veterinarians are under the impression that one cannot begin training a dog until the dog reaches adolescence or adulthood. They believe that a short attention span also means limited learning ability.

The fact is that dogs begin learning from the time of birth. They learn how to obtain their food, what smells and sounds signal that it's time to feed and how to solicit the giving of food from their mother. Much is instinct, but there is more that is learned through trial and error.

Puppies should begin formal training on the first day that they go to their new homes. Responsible breeders start the training process from the time of weaning. The pups learn to come to their food dishes on a specific cue. Many pups learn to relieve themselves in a specific area, if provided. The pups are exposed to various stimuli to prevent fear behaviors. Even those pups that don't have the benefit of being raised by a responsible breeder will learn behaviors from their mother, siblings and environment.

A new puppy owner should not give the pup time to acclimate to his new environment prior to beginning the pup's training. This merely allows the pup to develop bad habits and then to receive punishment at a later time for those behaviors that were allowed previously. This isn't fair to the pup. Why should he be punished for breaking rules that he was never really taught in the first place?

The rules should be set from day one. Pups are quite able to learn basic commands at the tender age of two months. By three months of age, their brains are fully formed and very open to learning. In fact, their brains are soaking up the stimuli of their environments like sponges. At this age, they are desirous of remaining with their new pack members (their owners) and will rarely stray too far.

Most pups learn quickly to come to the food bowl and dive right in—literally!

A challenge that every puppy owner faces is keeping the pup's attention. A toy is a good way to bring the pup's focus back to you.

These early behaviors can be tapped and enhanced to prevent future behavioral and training problems and to raise the pup in a positive manner. By using consistency from the beginning, using clear communication and working with the pup in five-minute increments throughout each day, the result is a canine companion that knows only proper behavior and learns quickly in any situation.

Puppy Training in 5 Minutes will teach you how to use canine communication skills to work with a very young puppy. You will then learn how to work within a pup's short attention span and accomplish new behaviors with each five-minute training session. This book will address common puppy behavioral issues, overall puppy care, puppy training and how to prevent future behavioral problems. The training procedures are based purely on positive reinforcement through treats, toys, touch and praise. These methods encourage a pup to perform specific behaviors through play. The procedures in this book will help you to develop a great puppy who will give you years of pleasure and companionship.

Happy training!

A puppy is truly a new family member, almost like a new baby or a new sibling to the kids.

KNOW YOUR PUPPY

Getting a puppy is similar to bringing home a new baby. Granted, you don't have to go through pregnancy or labor with a puppy, unless you're the dog's breeder, but you will have to change your life a bit and take the time to turn your puppy into a well-behaved member of the family. As you research what it means to become a puppy owner, you will notice that everyone has an opinion. What's more, everyone has a different opinion. Even worse, everyone has a different and conflicting opinion. Who's giving the advice you should follow? What will be the right thing to do?

There are many ways to raise a dog. Dogs are versatile, loyal and forgiving. They rarely hold grudges and are always willing to learn. The old adage, "You can't teach an old dog new tricks" does not ring true for dogs, only for closed-minded people. The best advice: keep an open mind. Ask questions. Try things. Use whatever works best for you and your puppy.

There are many sensible ways that will help you raise this new four-legged child. The first is to be consistent. Always do things the same way. Dogs are creatures of habit. If you are consistent, your pup will learn faster and will listen no matter where you are or what is going on around you. The second is to follow the three P's of training: *patience*, *persistence* and *praise*. Exercising the three P's will get you all the results you desire.

Puppies have an average attention span of approximately five minutes, some shorter, some longer. It is possible to increase a pup's attention span, but you will be most successful if you work with your puppy for five minutes at a time, followed by a rest period. Doing this several times a day will achieve results. Your pup will love to work and will gradually increase his attention span, and you will quickly accomplish all of the goals you have in mind for your puppy.

You might ask, "How can my puppy learn what he needs in just five minutes?" Easily. Use the techniques outlined in this book and you will be successful. Be consistent. Be patient. Be persistent. And praise your puppy whenever he does something good, even if it's a little thing.

One of the things that makes dogs one of the most popular pets in the world is their versatility. They can learn to exist in any environment and are ultimately social, intelligent creatures. If you take the time to work with your pup and guide him in the right direction, you will soon have a companion that fits you and your lifestyle.

Knowing as much as you can about where your pup comes from, such as his parentage (breed), early education (kennel where he was born and kept),

medical records and nutrition will aid the pup's transition into your life. Different breeds have different tendencies toward specific behavior patterns and physical needs. There are many exceptions to the rule, but one can make generalities. If you obtain your pup from a responsible breeder, you can usually be assured of a healthy pup that is typical of his breed and therefore should have certain behavioral characteristics that will help you anticipate his actions and prevent misunderstandings. Let's examine some of the general characteristics of the different groups of dogs, using AKC classification as the basis.

The whole family must devote time to the pup, caring for him and being consistent in what he is taught.

Golden Retrievers are good representatives of the Sporting Group. These are active, outdoor-loving dogs that certainly aren't afraid to get their paws wet.

GENERAL BEHAVIORS WITHIN BREED GROUPS

SPORTING GROUP

This group includes the pointers, retrievers, setters and spaniels, as well as the Vizsla and Weimaraner, two all-purpose hunting breeds. Sporting dogs were originally bred to aid hunters. From flushing and fetching to pointing and chasing, sporting dogs are bred for specific hunting conditions and types of game. These breeds have lots of energy, are very loyal and are eager to please. They love people and activities. Most sporting dogs make great family pets because of their ease in training and love of doing things with their owners. They do not do well in homes with children under five years of age, for they are too active and may inadvertently knock small children over, but they can keep up with well-behaved older children for well into their senior years.

Sporting breeds are often very friendly and eager to be part of the family unit. They do not do well if cooped up in small areas for long periods of time or left alone without a chance to play with other dogs and people. They require lots of exercise and do not care about the weather conditions as much as some other breeds. Most, in fact, have been bred to

The smallest of the Hound Group is the Miniature Dachshund.

retrieve from the water, so they don't understand why they cannot go out to play on a rainy day. They are high-energy and very demanding of attention. You had better love outdoor activities if you own a sporting dog!

HOUND GROUP
Hounds were some of the first known hunting dogs developed. The Hound Group consists of the

A popular working dog is the Siberian Husky. This Nordic sled dog is known for his endurance and helpfulness to man.

scenthound breeds (like the Bloodhound and Basset Hound), which locate and catch prey by scent, and the sighthound breeds (like the Greyhound and Irish Wolfhound), which locate and catch prey by sight. They have been specialized into trackers for locating prey and are rarely used for flushing, retrieving and pointing. Hounds will often follow a trail, regardless of any distraction, even that of their owners calling them to come. These breeds can be energetic, bold and stubborn, a combination often difficult to train. It is rare, however, to find an aggressive dog in this group. They all require consistent and patient training and must learn at an early age to always come when called, regardless of an interesting scent or sight, which poses quite a challenge. The sighthounds are especially known for their speed, and they can be off and running in a flash.

While your hound pup might be absolutely adorable when he jumps up and barks, this behavior will not be as cute when he is an adult dog. Starting him off right with proper training and behavior modification techniques as outlined in this book will ensure you of a pleasant companion. As a pup, your hound will have lots of energy, but he will mellow with age, turning into the dog that naps at your feet. Most hounds live well with children of all ages.

WORKING GROUP

These breeds were developed for a variety of tasks from guarding, herding and pulling to carrying loads and search-and-rescue. They can adapt to any temperatures and exhibit extreme intelligence and working abilities. Working-breed dogs can make great pets if fully integrated into their family packs. However, if left alone for long periods, chained up or constantly kenneled without any interaction, they can become dangerously aggressive. Some of these breeds were originally bred as fighting dogs, making them dangerous to have around children or small pets due to their high prey drive.

Playing tug-of-war with your working-breed puppy and hearing him growl as he pulls may be lots of fun, but you should refrain from these kinds of games until your pup has a better understanding of the family hierarchy and you are sure he knows his place in the pack. Inadvertently allowing your working-breed pup to "win" at this game can make him more assertive with family members as he grows. While some working-breed dogs do well with children if raised with them, you should only consider owning one of these breeds with children over the age of ten. Many of these dogs grow to be large, and a young child can easily be injured by a big, active dog, albeit accidentally.

TERRIER GROUP

Bred for hunting small game such as rodents, rabbits and foxes, terriers are tenacious and high-energy, rebelling against authority and showing aggression more easily than any other breed group. When riled, they do not back down easily. However, they do learn quickly and, if given proper guidance, socialization and obedience training, make great pets.

Due to a terrier's tenacious nature, it will be very important to involve your dog in as many social activities with other dogs and people as possible. Without

The Parson Russell Terrier is an energetic small terrier, known for being smart, quick and packed with personality.

The American Staffordshire Terrier is one of the "bull-and-terrier" breeds, members of the Terrier Group.

The Chihuahua is a toy dog with a giant personality.

this exposure, he can become aggressive toward strangers and other animals. Never praise your terrier for any type of growling and refrain from playing tug-of-war with him, for this increases his prey drive to dangerous levels. Games of fetch are the most productive. Also, you will need to practice removing things from your dog's mouth and replacing them with alternative objects. A terrier can become possessive/aggressive if allowed to steal and keep an off-limits item, and he must be taught to let go when you try to take the object away.

TOY GROUP

Most of the toy breeds were developed from the other major dog groups, their behaviors similar to the breeds from which they were derived. Toys acclimate easily to any living space and, due to their small size, do not require much space to receive proper exercise. Most of these breeds have house-training problems; however, this is due more to their being spoiled than to their own stubbornness, although that can be part of the problem. If not trained, toy breeds tend to bark excessively and are easily aggravated if they don't get what they want.

These dogs may be itty-bitty as pups, but they are still highly capable of learning everything taught to a larger-breed puppy. In fact, toys learn quickly, and they thoroughly enjoy the training interaction. A trained toy dog is an incredible companion. One of the many jobs available to a trained toy dog is therapy work. The size of the dog makes him very portable and appealing.

HERDING GROUP

This is generally known as one of the more intelligent breed groups. However, high intellect does not always make for a good pet. Herding breeds also have high energy levels and require constant stimulation. These types of dogs do not always work well in homes with young children, for they have a tendency to race after

One of the most popular and recognizable toy breeds in the world is the beautiful Yorkshire Terrier, famous for his blue and tan locks.

These irresistible balls of fluff are young Australian Shepherds, part of the Herding Group. The Aussie is a top choice of both farmers and pet owners due to his sharp instincts, intelligence and trainability; further, he is a top contender in many areas of the dog sport.

The Dalmatian, a member of the Non-Sporting Group, can certainly be "spotted" wherever he goes.

running youngsters, as though herding sheep, and can possibly knock them over.

Herding breeds are consistently among the top competitors in agility trials. Their intelligence allows them to quickly learn to navigate the obstacles, and their athleticism allows them to virtually fly through the course with speed and ease.

NON-SPORTING GROUP

These dogs are mainly companion dogs and, due to great variances between these breeds in size, looks, background, ability and temperament, one cannot make blanket statements about the behavioral attributes of these breeds. Breeds in this group range from the small Lhasa Apso to the large Standard Poodle, with many sizes, personalities and types in between.

RARE BREEDS

Aside from the breeds classified in the seven AKC groups, there are many rare breeds known in the US and around the world. In fact, some of the breeds that are considered "rare breeds" are quite popular as pets, with devoted followings. Of course, these breeds do not fall into one category, and it is impossible to make generalizations about them. However, when researching breeds, you may find a rare-breed gem that's perfect for you and your lifestyle.

The Perdiguero Portugese (Portuguese Pointer) is recognized by Europe's Fédération Cynologique Internationale in their Group 7, Pointing Dogs, but is a very rare breed in the US.

BASIC TEMPERAMENT TESTING FOR PUPPIES

Should you be obtaining a dog for a specific purpose, whether as a companion with whom to play fetch or as a dog that might work in search-and-rescue, you should put the puppy candidate through the Puppy Aptitude Test (PAT), developed by Joachim and Wendy Volhard, to make sure he has potential for what you have in mind. This type of testing is also important if you live with small children, disabled family members or elderly parents. The last thing you need is a pup that doesn't fit into your lifestyle.

The PAT should be performed

In the social
attraction test,
the tester claps
to get the pup's
attention.

in a quiet environment, away from the noises and distractions of the litter and other dogs on the premises. You must have the pup's undivided attention in order to obtain valid results. If possible, arrange with the breeder or rescue group from whom you are obtaining the pup to come visit the pup at five weeks of age and again at seven weeks of age to perform the test both times. Two weeks of puppy peer interaction can totally change the results.

The PAT evaluates behaviors including social attraction, following, restraint, social dominance, elevation dominance, retrieving, touch sensitivity, sound sensitivity and sight sensitivity. Each individual test within the PAT will give you a good idea of your candidate's aptitude as a pet and for specific tasks.

TEST 1: SOCIAL ATTRACTION
Place your pup in the test area. As you back a few feet away from the area's entrance, try to coax him toward you. You can clap your hands, kneel down and use an inviting tone of voice.
Reactions:
1. Came readily, tail up, jumped and bit at your hands.
2. Came readily, tail up, pawed and licked at your hands.
3. Came readily, tail up.
4. Came readily, tail down.
5. Came with hesitation, tail down.
6. Did not come at all.

TEST 2: FOLLOWING

Stand up and walk away from the pup in a normal manner. Don't run or walk too slowly. Make sure that the pup sees you walk away. The purpose of this is to test the degree of following attraction. A puppy that follows will be a dog that will be social and want to work for you.

Reactions:

1. Followed readily, tail up, got underfoot, bit at your feet.
2. Followed readily, tail up, got underfoot.
3. Followed readily, tail up.
4. Followed hesitantly, tail down.
5. Did not follow.
6. Went in the opposite direction.

TEST 3: RESTRAINT

Crouch down and gently roll the pup onto his back, holding him with one hand for a full 30 seconds. This will test the degree of dominant or submissive tendency and how the pup accepts stress when socially/physically dominated.

Reactions:

1. Struggled fiercely, flailed and bit at your hands.
2. Struggled fiercely, flailed.
3. Settled, struggled, settled with some eye contact.
4. Struggled, then settled.
5. No struggle.
6. No struggle, strained to avoid eye contact.

This pup came readily and licked the tester's hands.

The elevation dominance test.

TEST 5: ELEVATION DOMINANCE
Bend over and cradle the pup under his chest. With your fingers interlaced and your palms up, elevate his front quarters just off the ground. Hold him there for 30 seconds. This will test how the puppy accepts or resists being in a position of no control.
Reactions:
1. Struggled fiercely, bit and growled.
2. Struggled fiercely.
3. No struggle, relaxed.
4. Struggled, settled, licked.
5. No struggle, licked at hands.
6. Froze.

TEST 4: SOCIAL DOMINANCE
Allow your puppy to stand up and gently stroke him from his head to his back while you crouch beside him. Continue stroking until a recognizable behavior is established. This will test the puppy's degree of accepting social dominance. The pup may try to dominate by jumping and nipping, or he may be independent and walk away.
Reactions:
1. Jumped, pawed, bit and growled.
2. Jumped, pawed.
3. Cuddled up to you and tried to lick your face.
4. Squirmed, licked at your hands.
5. Rolled over and licked at your hands.
6. Went away and remained away.

Stroking the pup during the social dominance test.

The pup retrieves a crumpled piece of paper. Desire to retrieve is a predictor of the pup's potential for certain types of training, including as a service dog or for competitive sports.

TEST 6: RETRIEVING

While this is a desired behavior in many dogs to be used for hunting, this is also one of the most important tests for a service dog, whether the dog is intended to aid the physically challenged or locate lost persons. Further, retrieving is also of extreme importance for most types of competitive canine sports.

Crouch beside your puppy and attract his attention with a crumpled-up paper ball. When he shows interest and is watching, toss the object four to six feet in front of him. You can also try throwing a soft ball or small bone. Reactions:

1. Chases object and runs away.
2. Chases object, stands over it and does not return.
3. Chases object and returns with the object.
4. Chases object and returns without the object.
5. Starts to chase the object, but loses interest.
6. Does not chase the object.

TEST 7: TOUCH SENSITIVITY

This test is of extreme importance should you wish to take your dog into hospitals and nursing homes for pet-therapy work. Often the residents are not aware of how to properly approach and/or pet a visiting canine, so the dog must be amiable and not spook if he is touched in a sensitive area.

Take one of the pup's front paws and press it lightly between your finger and thumb. Gently add pressure until the pup reacts by pulling away or showing discomfort. Reactions:

1. Eight to ten counts before response.
2. Six to seven counts before response.
3. Five to six counts before response.
4. Two to four counts before response.
5. One to two counts before response.
6. Immediate response.

TEST 8: SOUND SENSITIVITY

Passing this test will be very important for a therapy dog or one that will be shown in performance trials. It's also important if you have children, for they often run

Touching the pup's toes gauges how comfortable or uncomfortable he is with being handled in sensitive areas.

In the sound sensitivity test, this pup showed interest in, rather than fear of, the jangling keys.

The sight sensitivity test: this pup responds to the toy by going after it with no hesitation.

After the test, the puppy should be allowed to relax and play.

around noisily, displaying erratic behavior.

Place your pup in the center of your testing area. Someone other than you should make a loud, sharp noise, such as dropping a book or a set of keys. A large metal spoon struck sharply on a metal pan once or twice would also work well.

Reactions:
1. Listens, locates the sound and walks toward the sound, barking.
2. Listens, locates the sound and barks.
3. Listens, locates the sound and shows curiosity by walking toward the source of the sound.
4. Listens and locates the sound but does not move toward the source.
5. Cringes, backs off and hides.
6. Ignores the sound, shows no curiosity.

TEST 9: SIGHT SENSITIVITY

This test will give you an idea of the pup's intelligent response to a strange object. Place your puppy in the center of the testing area. Tie a string around a large towel or toy and jerk it across the enclosure, close to the dog.

Reactions:
1. Looks at the object, attacks it and bites at it.
2. Looks at the object and barks with his tail up.
3. Looks curiously and attempts to investigate or play with the object.
4. Looks, barks and tucks his tail.
5. Runs away and hides.
6. No reaction.

INTERPRETING THE PAT SCORES

The interpretation of the PAT scores is as follows:

Mostly 1s: This puppy is extremely dominant and has aggressive tendencies. He is quick to bite and is generally considered not to be a good candidate for a home with children or the elderly. When combined with a 1 or a 2 in the touch sensitivity test, he will most likely be a difficult puppy to train. This puppy would not be suggested for an inexperienced handler, for it takes a competent trainer to establish leadership and positive direction.

Mostly 2s: This puppy is dominant and can possibly be provoked to bite. He responds well to firm, consistent, fair handling in an adult household and is likely to be a loyal pet once he respects his human leader. This puppy often has a bouncy, outgoing temperament but may be too active for a home where there are children, disabled or elderly residents.

Mostly 3s: This puppy easily accepts humans as leaders. This type of pup is the best prospect for any job or lifestyle. A puppy scoring in this range would easily fit into a home where there are children and other activities. In fact, he would thrive on stimulating activities, such as agility, obedience training and fetching games, making him a good performance or service dog.

Handling a pup whose test results have shown him to be "independent."

Handling a puppy who has tested as an all-around good candidate, coming readily and being amenable to handling.

Puppy showing submissive expression.

Mostly 4s: This pup is submissive and will adapt to most households but should not be forced into "scary" situations. Time and patience are the keys. He may be slightly less outgoing and active than the previous type of puppy, but he generally gets along well with children and is easy to train. This puppy might make a good therapy dog, for he'll be calmer and more accepting of those with physical disabilities.

Mostly 5s: This puppy is extremely submissive and needs special handling to build confidence. A pup within this range of scores should not be put in a home with active children but may work out well in a quiet adult-only home or with the elderly. He will not adapt well to change and needs a very structured environment. A novice owner should not fall for his soulful eyes. This puppy will require lots of patience and the proper training approach; thus only an experienced dog owner should take him home.

Mostly 6s: This puppy is very independent. He is not affectionate and may dislike cuddling. It may be difficult to establish a relationship with him, whether as a working dog or as a pet. This is not a pup that should live with children or someone who is not an experienced dog owner. He may do well in a quiet home with little commotion. This is a pup that will prefer to lie near the fireplace or in the corner rather than to go out for a game of fetch. He might greatly enjoy walking in the woods, though he should be kept on a leash.

There are several variations on the scoring that might indicate some other behaviors. For example, a puppy scoring mostly 2s or 3s, but that has some 1s in the restraint tests, is likely to bite under stress. If the independent puppy also has some 5 scores, he is likely to hide from people or freeze when approached by a stranger. If there is no clear pattern to the scores, it is highly likely that the puppy is not feeling well or is so stressed by his current situation that you will not be able to obtain a clear picture of his "normal" behavior. In this case, you may want to try doing the test again a few days later.

STARTING OFF ON THE RIGHT PAW

So what if you're a lefty? I am too. That's not an excuse for not starting off on the right paw. The paw that will turn your pup into a fabulous companion. The paw that will assure your pup a long, healthy life. Regardless of which side of your brain is dominant, the right paw should take precedence in puppy training.

There is much to take into consideration when caring for your new puppy. He has to have proper nutrition, grooming, veterinary care and special attention paid to specific physical conditions. He must also have socialization and

proper mental stimulation. These things will allow him to grow into a healthy, happy dog.

PUPPY PREPARATIONS

You'll need to prepare your home for the new pup. You will also need to adjust your lifestyle for a while. Puppies are much like toddlers and need to be watched at all times to prevent injury to themselves or destruction of things in your home. Therefore the first order of business is to puppy-proof! Lift those knick-knacks to make them unreachable. Move

There's nothing like a cute puppy! Now's the time to make sure that he is taught to act as sweet as he looks.

The puppy must be introduced to new experiences in a positive manner. A favorite toy helps him associate bathtime with fun.

A wire exercise pen, or "ex-pen," is a helpful tool for safely confining your puppy, giving him a little more room to run than his crate.

Safe chew toys will keep a puppy happily occupied, with his teeth and mind diverted from chewing forbidden objects.

that garbage can. Clear off the coffee tables. Cover the electrical cords. Make a safe puppy area in the home and securely fence your yard.

If there's something dangling, tasty or tempting, your puppy will make a beeline for it. Keep lots of puppy toys around to replace the "bad" things with a "good" thing. The key term is *redirect*. When your pup takes or puts his mouth on something he's not supposed to have, show him a toy and play with him as you praise him. We'll speak more about that later. For now, make sure there's nothing within your pup's reach or in the areas to which he will have access that can cause him injury or illness. You may not have to worry so much about his hitting his head on the table edges as you would with a human toddler, but those table edges might be tempting to chew on. I suggest having some anti-chew spray handy, which will make a "tasty" object very

unpalatable if the pup attempts to take a bite.

Here's a list of items you'll need before bringing puppy home. You might wish for diapers at times, but they're not on this list!

• Crate. It's more economical to purchase a crate that will accommodate your pup at his full adult size, as puppies grow quickly. Depending on the breed, your pup may outgrow several crates before reaching adulthood, which will be quite costly! The solution is to use a divider panel to partition the crate into a puppy-sized area, gradually increasing the size of the area until the panel is no longer needed.

• Soft bed with a removable cover. You may want more than one cover so that one can be put on the bed while the other is being washed. Potty accidents will happen, so you may be doing

the wash more often than usual.
- Two dog dishes. I suggest bowls made from stainless steel because the material is not chewable or likely to break. These bowls last a long time and are easy to sanitize. If your pup likes to play in his water, get a pail that hooks to the side of the crate instead of putting his water on the floor. A water bottle that hangs on the crate and dispenses water as the pup drinks might also work.
- Soft brush for the puppy coat.
- Small canine toothbrush and canine toothpaste.
- Dental chews to massage the gums and keep the teeth clean.
- Adjustable collar and light-weight leash made of either cotton or leather. Stay away from chains, as you will not be able to use them during training. Why buy more than you'll need?
- Toys, toys and more toys. You may also want a box to put them in. Remember that puppy will be teething through nine

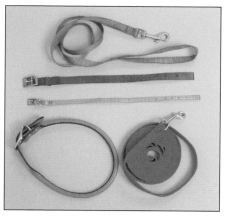

Nylon leashes come in many lengths. What you use will depend on the size of your dog and how well he walks on lead. Also shown are a rolled leather collar and a pair of nylon buckle collars.

months. He's better off teething on toys than on your couch.

Now that's thinking with the right side of the brain! See, it's great to be left-handed.

PROPER NUTRITION

While nursing from his mother, your pup received all the nutrients he needed to remain healthy. By the age of four weeks, however, the mother dog began to wean her pups and they began to eat solid food. Breeders begin feeding special puppy food that is higher in fat and protein than adult foods, although the optimal fat and protein content can vary greatly, depending on breed and size. The puppy diet is designed to make sure that the pups can maintain their growth and energy levels in a healthy manner.

Due to a pup's small stomach and high activity level, he should be fed three to four times per day. His metabolism acts quickly,

Start off with the basics for grooming a puppy: a soft bristle brush, a metal comb and a grooming glove.

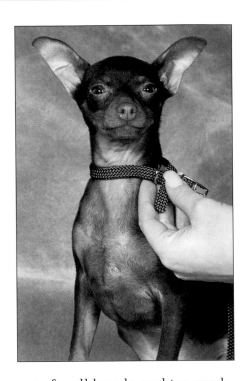

A puppy will be comfortable wearing a lightweight yet sturdy leash and collar.

sending the food through his system almost as fast as he eats it. Since he has small teeth, his food should be moistened with warm water or a bit of milk replacement formula. This also aids in his digestion of the food, for it will be partially broken down before it reaches his puppy stomach.

Many breeders have a preference for certain food brands, having researched what works well for their breeds and particular bloodlines. Unless your puppy is having digestive problems, stick to whatever brand he was eating prior to going home with you. A good breeder will send you home with details of the puppy's feeding and maybe even a small amount of the puppy food. If you have to choose the pup's food yourself, ask your veterinarian for nutrition advice and check the labels on the food bags before making a selection. In general, a good protein level for pups is from 33 to 43%, although this is definitely not the

Stainless steel bowls, puppy food and fresh water are the keys to a healthy diet for the youngster.

case for all breeds, and too much protein can actually be harmful. Again, it is necessary to discuss the puppy's food with your breeder and/or vet. In general, however, protein and fat levels will be higher in the puppy's diet as compared to the adult's diet, as this is necessary for normal growth and the production of antibodies to aid in a puppy's overall ability to fight infection and heal quickly.

A pup with a super-sensitive digestive system would do well on a chicken- or lamb-based meal. Check for fillers such as plant-source ingredients and ground by-products. Corn and wheat are very

A water-loving retriever may have other ideas for his bowl!

No matter how well fed, a puppy won't be able to resist rummaging for a treat. Keep trash cans closed and away from where the dog can get to them.

common ingredients, but many dogs have trouble digesting them. Other dogs develop allergies because of them. A premium food will not have these ingredients. While rice, barley and other grains as well as vegetables are good to help maintain overall vitamin balance, puppies need meat. They get most of their protein through sources such as chicken, fish meal, eggs and dairy products.

New puppy owners are often tempted to spoil their pups by offering table scraps or feeding them by hand. Don't fall into this trap. Your puppy needs the nutrients contained in dog food and must learn to eat out of his own dish. Be sure to feed your puppy at the same place and approximately at the same times of the day. Don't worry if he doesn't finish every meal. Feeding him unfinished portions by hand will only turn into a bad habit. Some

When it comes to food, don't baby your pup by hand-feeding him or offering table scraps. He must learn to eat from his bowl during his regular mealtimes.

puppies are hungrier after they've had a little exercise and therefore will eat better later in the day. Just be certain not to feed your puppy directly after exercise. This can cause digestive problems, especially if his genetics include a breed that has a propensity to bloat. These breeds are usually those with a large chest area such as the Weimaraner, Doberman Pinscher and even the Parson Russell Terrier. Do some research on the breed of your pup to ensure that you are feeding him correctly and safely. There are many simple preventives that you should incorporate into your dog's feeding and exercise routine if he may be prone to bloat; discuss this with your vet and breeder.

Puppies have a tendency to eat just about anything. While you're walking your puppy, he'll eat mulch, dirt, leaves, candy wrappers and cigarette butts, among other nasty things. This will often lead to gastrointestinal upset, which in turn will cause him to vomit or have diarrhea. First of all, keep a constant watch on where your pup's little nose travels. Take anything from his mouth that isn't an approved edible object. Should you notice gastrointestinal distress, take a stool sample to your veterinarian. A mild case of gastritis is easily treated by feeding a bland diet, such as boiled chicken or cottage cheese and rice, for a few days. Once your pup is feeling better, gradually, over the course of several days, return him to his normal food.

It's more serious if your dog has ingested a toxin. These include "people foods" like chocolate, nuts, grapes, raisins and onions, or any chemicals and fertilizers. Antifreeze is especially dangerous, and some mulch contains the same toxin found in chocolate. If your dog has ingested one of these, or even if you suspect he may have, contact your veterinarian.

Getting back to proper nutrition, periodically check your pup's weight. A young pup will be growing like a weed, but during his first three months he should still appear "roly poly." Examine your pup by running your hand along his sides and feeling for his ribs. You should barely be able to feel the ribs. There should be a slight indentation at his waist, and you should not be able to clearly feel or see his hip bones.

As your pup develops and matures, you can reduce his feed-

ing times to twice a day, in the morning and evening. With your young puppy, who needs to eat more frequently, you should try to enlist the help of a neighbor, family member or dogsitter to feed his midday meal if you are at work all day. It is important that a young pup eat more often. You should not reduce the frequency of his mealtimes until he is at least five months old, for his metabolism requires more frequent feedings in order to obtain appropriate nutrition. Also, giving him some vitamin supplements such as ester-C and vitamin E will help prevent possible growing pains, a common occurrence in fast-growing large-breed dogs. Before adding any type of supplementation, though, do consult your vet.

GROOMING
Even if your puppy doesn't have long hair, he still needs to learn about being groomed. In fact, he

A baby Lab pup is weighed on a scale. A large-breed pup has lots of growing to do but still starts out as small as any other pup.

Top view of a healthy puppy. A puppy should appear "roly-poly," meaning his body shape will not be the same as that of an adult, but he should not be obese.

You can bathe your pup in a bathtub or even the kitchen sink, using a mild shampoo made for dogs.

or tub with warm water.

Have all of your supplies ready. You should have special doggy shampoo, a dry towel, a toy and some treats. It would also be a good idea to place cotton balls in the puppy's ears to prevent moisture from entering the ear canal. Should you wish to thoroughly wash his face, put some ophthalmic ointment in his eyes to prevent irritation from the shampoo. If you are using puppy shampoo, however, his eyes shouldn't be irritated if some suds get into them.

You'll want to make the first bath a positive experience. This won't be a problem for some breeds, such as the water-loving

Have a heavy towel ready for when your pup is thoroughly rinsed and you're ready to lift him out of the basin.

may even be in need of a bath when you first bring him home. Have you thought about how you're going to do this? Certainly not with a garden hose and absolutely not outside. Puppies have a difficult time regulating their body temperatures. They need to be kept warm.

The best place to bathe your puppy for the first time would be the kitchen or laundry-room sink, or even the bathtub. This allows you to get on the same level with your pup and keep him in a smaller area for safety. The bottom of the basin should have a non-slip surface. This can be achieved with a rubber mat or by placing a towel down before filling the sink retrievers and spaniels. However, for others, no matter what you do, they will still shake and pout. While he's being bathed, you should give your puppy lots of praise and a treat now and then. You can float a toy in the water, such as a squeaky rubber duck. This will make for a fun and positive experience.

You will need to bathe your puppy every ten days to two weeks (don't worry, you will bathe him much less frequently as he grows up). Puppies are close to the ground and love to roll in stinky things. Frequent bathing will keep him from getting a doggy odor and make him more pleasant to hug. Be sure to only use a shampoo made for dogs to prevent his skin from drying out. The natural oils in his coat are important for protection from the elements. Further, a shampoo that dries his skin will cause severe itching and irritation, reducing his ability to fight bacteria.

Always make sure you thoroughly dry your pup after his bath. Never let him go outside while still wet. Puppies can easily catch a chill, which further lowers their resistance to airborne bacteria and viruses.

Establish a brushing routine with your pup. Not only does regular brushing help you notice anything abnormal with the skin and coat, it also helps with bonding. Brushing regularly removes loose hair, eliminates tangles and distributes skin oil. Begin the brushing routine from day one. A longhaired pup will need brushing every day. A shorthaired breed will require brushing only once or twice weekly, but it does not hurt to give your pup a quick once-over whenever he is exposed to an environment that might harbor parasites, such as woods and meadows with high grass. During the warm months, ticks and fleas are abundant. In the fall, plants shed seeds in the form of burs. These can irritate soft pads and sensitive skin. Remove them immediately.

The type of brush you use should be soft. Most puppies

Heavily coated breeds like the Poodle certainly look a lot different when wet!

The Maltese as a puppy has a much different coat than as an adult. The fluffy puppy coat changes into the straight, long, silky coat of the adult.

All family members can help with the dog's grooming. The Eurasier is a rare breed with a dense coat. His young friend is using a soft brush.

aren't ready for rakes, combs and slickers. Their skin is sensitive and their coats still short. To ensure that your pup has a good experience with grooming, use flexible bristle brushes and grooming gloves. Take your time and allow your pup to enjoy the attention. Do his grooming when he's tired and relaxing. Your pup will be less likely to turn his grooming into a game if he's not in "play" mode.

Begin by brushing your pup's head and ears, then do his chest and front legs, back, sides, tummy and hindquarters. Finish up with his tail. Brush gently, but firmly enough to make sure that all loose hair and dander is removed. Until your pup is very used to being brushed, always brush only in the direction in which his hair grows.

The toenails will need attention every six to eight weeks. Canine toenails can be very sharp and easily shred fabric or cut your skin. Puppy nails, in particular, are sharp and grow quickly. It's a good idea to get your pup used to the nail-clipping process as early as possible. He needs to remain absolutely still while this is done. At first you might want someone to help you hold him while you trim the nails so that you can concentrate on not trimming too short. Cutting into the pink part (known as the quick) of his nail will cause severe bleeding as well as give your puppy a negative association with having his nails clipped.

Look closely at the nail. It will appear similar in shape to a hawk's beak. The best place to trim is a quarter inch before the sharp curve in the nail. Above this curve will be the pulpy part of the nail, similar to the pink part of your own nails. Below this is the clear part (end) of the nail. This is the safe place to trim. Should your puppy have black nails, making it difficult to see where to trim, clip off just a little at a time until you are close to where the nail curves. Always file the nail with an emery board or hand-held rotary tool to round it off.

Ear cleaning is also required for your pup's overall health, espe-

Puppies and small dogs can be made comfortable on their owners' laps during nail clipping.

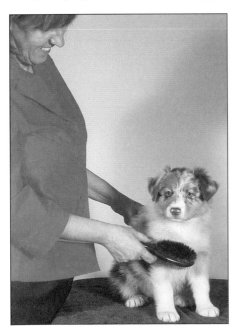

cially if your puppy is the type with floppy ears. Floppy ears don't allow good air circulation to dry out excess moisture. If your puppy is a retriever, his ear canals may be narrow, further trapping bacteria and moisture. Trapped moisture can cause an ear infection. Some infections are caused by mites, others by yeast and dirt build-up. A weekly cleaning will ensure that your pup's ears remain clean and healthy. The last thing you want to deal with is frequent ear infections, which can not only cause your puppy much discom-

The Australian Shepherd does not have a long coat, but it is a heavy coat. The Aussie enjoys time outdoors and should be brushed and checked often to keep his coat free of mats and debris.

A cotton swab can be used for ear cleaning, but be careful not to probe into the ear canal and to keep the puppy sitting still.

Some pups in some breeds, like the Boxer, have their ears cropped at an early age. Cropped ears require special aftercare on the part of the owners.

fort but can also eventually cause deafness from repeated damage to his middle ear.

An ear infection is pretty easy to spot. The puppy will shake his head a lot, rubbing his ears on the floor and furniture, and you will detect an unpleasant odor in his ears. Should this occur, immediately take your puppy to your veterinarian for treatment.

There are many ear-cleaning products on the market, but you can also use mineral oil. Place a bit of the fluid on a soft rag. Gently clean the outer ear, taking special care around the features. To clean a little deeper, put some fluid on a cotton swab, but never probe into the ear canal. Keep all your attention on the outer ears only. Your veterinarian is the only one who should clean your pup's inner ears.

Some dogs have a lot of hair in their ears. These fine hairs can

disrupt air flow, trapping dirt and moisture. Most puppies don't have this yet, but be prepared to take a pair of tweezers to the insides of the ears when your dog is fully grown. Pull only the hairs that come out easily, as this is painless for the dog. Don't pull stubborn hairs, as this will make your pup cry out and remind him of how painful the experience can be if done incorrectly. Remember, you want to keep everything as positive as possible.

Regular eye cleaning will also be important for dogs with protruding eyes, such as the Pomeranian, Chihuahua, Lhasa Apso and Shih Tzu. Should you see discharge or redness, this could mean either an irritation or infection. A saline eye solution can be used once a week to keep the eyes clear. Always check for dirt particles and hair in the eyes.

Trimming the hair around the eyes will be helpful in keeping them clear. Dogs of many breeds can be prone to tear staining, so, regardless of breed, make sure the area around your dog's eyes is kept free of stains, dirt and debris.

Something most dog owners ignore is dental hygiene. Many people think that giving their dogs hard biscuits is sufficient, but this is not the case. While biscuits do help reduce tartar buildup, they do not effectively rid the teeth of plaque and tartar. Your pup's gums will also need attention to prevent future periodontal disease.

Even though your pup only has his baby teeth, you should begin brushing at least twice per week. Granted, his baby teeth do fall out, but you want to acclimate him to the process itself, not just the matter of keeping his teeth clean and breath fresh.

Regular brushing will avoid those trips to the veterinarian to have the teeth scaled. It will also help prolong his life in many ways. First of all, he will keep his teeth longer, which means he'll be able to properly chew his food. Second, it will prevent periodontal disease, an infection of the gums. Periodontal disease not only causes teeth to fall out but also transfers bacteria to his internal organs, reducing their efficiency. While you may not see these problems while your dog is young, they will arise later in his life, so it's a good idea to begin the dental-care routine early on.

Small breeds tend to require more dental attention than larger breeds. Even though you may clean your pup's teeth regularly,

Dogs with protruding eyes, like the Shih Tzu, need special attention to eye care.

Young English Springer Spaniel pups are being accustomed to having their faces examined.

he may still need to occasionally have his teeth professionally scaled. Your veterinarian will have to anesthetize him so that he can gain easier access to every tooth. However, brushing regularly will decrease the frequency with which you have to put your dog through this stressful situation.

Smaller breeds also have a tendency to experience trouble getting rid of their baby teeth. Keep a watchful eye out for doubled teeth, especially the incisors. This can cause eating disorders and even grouchiness, as your pup will be in pain from a dying tooth that won't dislodge from his gums.

For toothbrushing, you can use a child's toothbrush, a finger brush or contoured toothbrush (both specially manufactured for cleaning canine teeth) or even a

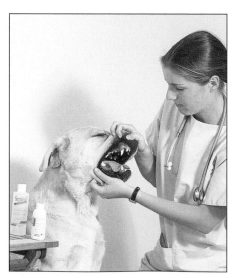

In order to receive proper dental care, a dog must be amenable to having his mouth handled.

soft washcloth. Put some doggie toothpaste (this comes in various flavors) on the surface of your implement and clean each tooth in a circular motion, including the gums around the tooth. Your pup may give you problems in cleaning his lower teeth. Be patient and aim for one at a time. Allow him a breather every so often. Take a few days to accomplish a complete dental cleaning, doing one tooth at a time. Your pup will gradually become used to the process and learn to accept it, even look forward to it, for the flavored toothpaste is a treat.

PUPPY VETERINARY CARE
Proper veterinary care should begin as soon as you bring your pup home. In fact, you might want to make a stop at the veterinarian's office on the way home from picking up your pup. If not, an appointment should be set up for sometime within the next few days. A thorough health check might catch something you hadn't noticed previously. This is especially important if you have other pets at home.

The following vaccination guidelines represent those commonly used. Inoculation schedules and recommendations can vary according to the individual dog and region where you live, so discuss your pup's course of vaccines with your vet to ensure safe and complete protection.

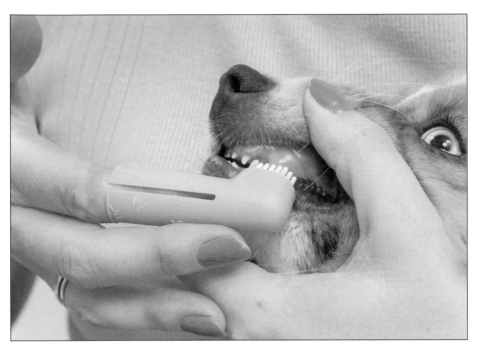

A convenient type of doggie toothbrush fits right over the owner's finger.

It will take some coaxing to hold a pup still while administering eye drops.

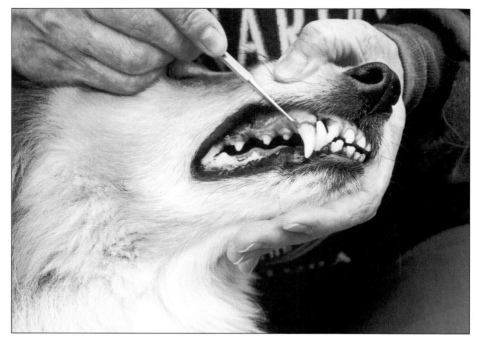

Your vet will likely do a thorough tooth-scraping as part of your dog's annual exam.

His first inoculation should be at six weeks of age. Most breeders will do this along with the first two wormings. This is followed by a series of boosters, the rabies vaccine and a kennel cough inhalant, which are your responsibility. It will be up to you to take your pup to the vet to continue with his vaccinations where the breeder left off. By the time your pup is four months old (or five months old, depending on your local rabies-vaccine law), he should have everything he needs to fight the most common canine infections. With yearly boosters, he'll maintain his immunity.

There are some breeds that might be sensitive to yearly boost-ers; with these dogs, it might be safer to have a titer test done instead. A titer test is a blood test that checks for appropriate levels of vaccine and resistance to specific viruses. If vaccine levels are sufficient, it may not be necessary to revaccinate. Titer tests are becoming more common in communities where dogs are not exposed to the wilds of rural areas. Titer tests cannot be done on puppies, however, as they have yet to develop their immunities through regular vaccinations.

Your pup's first three vaccines will be combination shots, called "all-in-one" vaccines. This is the preferred method, as it involves only one shot instead of five to deliver the medication. This all-in-one inoculation vaccinates against parvovirus, leptospirosis, hepatitis, parainfluenza and canine distemper. Some even include coronavirus vaccine, a virus to which puppies are very susceptible.

Parvovirus and coronavirus are diseases that attack the intestinal tract, white blood cells and heart muscles. These diseases are very contagious. Young puppies are very susceptible to airborne contagions and can respond violently to parvovirus through heart failure. Left untreated, it can be fatal.

Leptospirosis is a bacterial disease that is transmitted by contact with either the urine of an infected dog or objects contaminated by the urine of an infected dog. This disease can result in kidney failure, which is why it's best to prevent your pup from going to a dog park or playing with other canines until he has received all of his vaccines. Contact with a dog that you know well should be fine, provided that you are aware of the other dog's health background.

Hepatitis is a disease that attacks a pup's liver. Sometimes a pup can get a respiratory infection as a secondary symptom. As with leptospirosis, contact with the urine or objects touched by the urine of an infected animal transmits the disease to the immune-deficient puppy.

Parainfluenza is not as fatal as the previously described infections but can cause much discomfort. Should your pup have contact with the nasal secretions of a dog with this virus, he can show symptoms of upper respiratory distress such as sneezing, nasal discharge and overall lethargy. Many stray dogs contract this infection due to their contact with other unprotected canines.

Canine distemper is spread not only through contact with the nasal secretions of infected dogs but also through contact with ocular (eye) secretions. This virus can also be carried on air currents or on inanimate objects. First, the affected dog would show respiratory distress and flu-like symptoms. Should he not be treated in

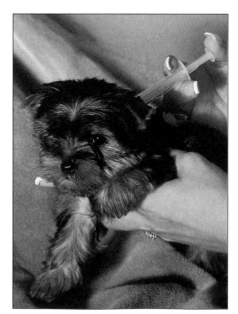

Your vet will manage the details of your pup's vaccination schedule once the pup comes home with you.

time, distemper can be fatal. This is another infection commonly seen in dogs that have been stray for long periods of time.

There are two other vaccines that you should talk to your vet about. One is a vaccine against Lyme disease, and the other is the *Giardia* vaccine. Lyme disease is transmitted through tick bites. Should you live in an area where ticks are prevalent, which is everywhere nowadays, make sure your pup has this yearly inoculation. Lyme disease creeps into your dog's system. It first causes achy muscles and lethargy but eventually can cause complete paralysis and death. However, there are some breeds of dog, such as Collies and the other herding breeds, that react poorly to this vaccine. In any case, remain vigilant about your pup's exposure to wooded or bushy areas. Using a topical repellent can also be very helpful.

Giardia bacteria affect the gastrointestinal system. All dogs are very susceptible to these bacteria, especially puppies. The symptoms include mucousy diarrhea and vomiting. *Giardia* is contracted through drinking infected water, which is commonly found in ponds, streams, lakes and rivers that derive their sources from farmland or woodland areas. Usually mountain water sources are fairly clean, but have been known to contain

the bacteria. If you take your pup for walks in the country, always be aware of what he eats and drinks. Giving him the *Giardia* vaccine will be helpful in preventing a mess in your house and a regression in house-training.

Your pup can't tell you how he's feeling, so you'll have no way of knowing if he's ill other than by observing his behavior and watching for symptoms. Make sure that you cover all of the bases. Get the pup's first set of shots right away. This first set includes vaccines for distemper, hepatitis, parvovirus and parainfluenza. Two weeks later, your pup should receive his next set, which includes boosters for distemper, hepatitis, parvovirus and parainfluenza, as well as his first leptospirosis inoculation. After another two weeks, he again receives boosters for all of his previous inoculations. The all-important rabies vaccine is given at an age determined by state or local law, then again a year later. In the case of a dog over the specified age, the rabies shot is given immediately. After the first booster, the rabies vaccine won't have to be repeated until three to five years later, depending on the type used. However, all other vaccines will need yearly boosters unless you have the titer test and it shows that the boosters are unnecessary.

If you plan on attending a group training class or boarding

your pup in a kennel at any time, you should request that he receive the *Bordetella* vaccine. This vaccine is usually done through a nasal spray, administered directly into the nose. The *Bordetella* vaccine guards against two strains of kennel cough, a highly contagious respiratory illness. The symptoms include coughing and nasal secretions. Without treatment, it can blossom into a worse problem, such as bronchitis.

Ask your veterinarian to also begin your pup on a parasite-control regimen. This includes heartworm prevention and flea control. There are many different products currently on the market to aid dog owners in battling these parasites. Heartworm infestation is a very serious problem and, if not caught in time, can prove fatal. You can begin your pup on heartworm preventive as early as eight weeks of age. There are several different types of chewable tablets available, many of which offer not only heartworm, hookworm and whipworm prevention but also flea control. All of this in one monthly chewable tablet!

Should you already be dealing with a flea infestation, or regularly taking your pup to places where fleas are present, you'll want to use a topical solution to both repel and kill fleas. Puppies tend to do well with spot-on treatments. These products are applied directly onto the skin between

Collies and other herding breeds do not handle the Lyme disease vaccine well; they also should not be given parasite medication containing Ivermectin. It is helpful if your chosen vet is knowledgeable about your breed.

your pup's shoulder blades. They are specially formulated to not harm a young pup's tender skin. As your puppy grows, you can switch to one of the products that offers coverage against ticks and even mosquitoes as well as fleas. Some of these products are suitable for use from puppyhood throughout the dog's life.

Another product has combined both flea prevention and heartworm prevention into a topical application. It is applied between the shoulder blades and, in the case of a dog larger than 33 pounds, at the base of the tail, once per month. This will protect against fleas and many types of worm infestation while also repelling brown dog ticks. However, it does not repel deer

A handshake from this Great Pyrenees would not be so friendly if his dewclaws and toenails were not trimmed properly.

ticks, the carriers of Lyme disease. It may also not protect against mosquitoes as it wears off.

SPECIAL NEEDS OF SPECIFIC BODY TYPES

Each breed has its own idiosyncrasies. Dewclaw care, anal sac maintenance and attention to respiratory problems in brachycephalic (short-nosed) breeds are common. Toy dogs are very susceptible to weather extremes and cannot be outside for too long when the temperatures are very hot or very cold. Their overall size makes it difficult for them to regulate their body temperatures. While outdoors in the winter, they should wear some type of covering; during hot summer days, they cannot be left outdoors during midday heat. Those breeds with protruding eyes must receive special attention to their eyes due

to their susceptibility to foreign particles entering the eyes.

There are several breeds that have skin folds. The English Bulldog, Shar-Pei and Sussex Spaniel are but a few. If your puppy is one of or a mix of these breeds, his skin may tend to be dry on the outside of the folds, but moist on the inside. Particles of dirt can get inside the folds. Left alone, this can cause skin irritations. You should do a regular cleaning of all skin folds to ensure against topical infections and other irritations.

Many breeds are prone to skin allergies. This is best managed by offering help from the inside out. Under a vet's advice, you can supplement the diet with vitamin E and other amino acids via one of the several supplements available in many pet stores. These products will help your dog's skin to remain soft and his coat glossy. Should you see little red pimples, blotches or loss of hair, consult your veterinarian. He'll most likely place your dog on a special diet and prescribe medication to cure a possible infection. Puppies are very susceptible to bacterial and viral infections that manifest themselves on the skin.

Many large breeds of dog have large dewclaws on their front and/or hind feet. The Great Pyrenees and Saint Bernard are examples. The dewclaws will need nail maintenance on the same schedule as the other nails. An ignored dewclaw will result in the nail's curling under and possibly getting caught on something, resulting in injury. Keep in mind that the dewclaw is actually like a finger. It does have tissue and nerve endings, making any injury very painful.

Some dogs tend to have anal sac problems. This is more common in small breeds. The anal sacs are located on either side of the dog's anus. They contain fluids that are used when a dog is marking territory or exhibiting an emotion, such as fear. If impacted, the anal sacs cause great discomfort. Your pup might rub his rear end on the ground or lick the area under his tail. An impaction can become very smelly, and expressing the sacs is even more odoriferous. The best means of ensuring healthy anal sacs is to have your veterinarian or groomer express them regularly. Supplementing your pup's food with pumpkin and/or sweet potato, again under advice of your vet, helps prevent impaction of the anal glands. These foods are high in fiber, offering better gastrointestinal health.

There are many breeds that require special respiratory considerations. They have been bred to have shortened muzzles, which in turn reduces their ability to maintain their temperatures through their nasal passages. These breeds include the Boxer, Bulldog, Shih Tzu, Pug, Pekingese and Lhasa Apso. You must make sure to never allow a dog of this type to overheat. Heat exhaustion, if not treated immediately, can be fatal. On hot, humid days, it's best to keep them indoors as much as possible.

KEEPING YOUR PUPPY BUSY

Mental stimulation comes in the form of toys, games and training. Keeping puppy busy will keep him occupied and curb him from becoming destructive. Offer your puppy at least six different types of toys. Choose safe, durable toys that are appropriate for your dog's size. A too-large toy will be useless for a small dog, while a too-small toy will be dangerous to a large dog, as it can easily be swallowed. However, a word of advice about rawhide: let your pup have only large bones. When the bones become small or if he tears off a small chunk, throw it away. Little pieces of flat rawhide

The Pug is a popular example of a short-faced breed. These breeds may have breathing difficulties and need special care not to become overheated.

or rawhide sticks can easily lodge in the roof of his mouth or throat, causing him to choke. Also, rawhide is not digestible. Puppies have sensitive digestive systems. If your pup receives a lot of rawhide, he can vomit or have diarrhea. Keep the rawhide bone as a special once-in-a-while treat.

Bones ✴

In addition to chew toys, there are edible chews available. These are hard bones, made of vegetable matter, that are completely edible and digestible. Your puppy will enjoy an edible chew as much as he would a hard nylon chew bone or a rawhide bone. However, just as with anything edible, you don't want to overdo it, as too many edible chews can upset his tummy. Keep them to a minimum for special treats.

Small dogs will enjoy squeaky toys, chew bones, stuffed toys and rubber toys. Regardless of the toy and the size of the dog, your pup will be more enthusiastic about it if you play with him.

✴ *Teething*

For teething, try the following: Soak a few old washcloths in water, twist them and freeze them. Your pup will love to chew on one of these, as it helps relieve the discomfort of his teething. A frozen shank bone will also do the trick as well as any of the numerous toys on the market that offer this type of relief for pups. Ice cubes are fun, too. If you want to make a special treat, make puppy popsicles by filling an ice-cube tray with some chicken or beef bouillon. Voila! Homemade frozen treats.

In order to maintain your pup's interest in his toys, rotate them daily. Present him with three toys one day and a different three toys the next day. Each time, his reaction will be, "Oh boy! New toys!" This is much better than his deciding that your couch cushions or chair legs might be fun to play with.

The best means of keeping pup stimulated is to train him and teach him tricks. Puppies love learning, especially if it involves getting special rewards and praise. Don't wait until your pup "settles in." He'll settle in much faster if you begin training him right away. Puppies as young as five weeks are able to comprehend and respond to commands. You won't have your puppy at that young age, but you will essentially be starting with a clean slate and a mind that soaks up everything like a sponge. Waiting until later will mean having to overcome already-established behavioral problems and facing a resistant adolescent. A new home is a place for the pup to begin learning about his environment, a big part of which is learning what is and what is not allowed. Begin right away and your puppy will be easier to work with as he gets older and enters adolescence.

GET TO KNOW THE SCHEDULE

Most puppies have to relieve themselves very often. The smaller the breed, the less capacity in the bladder and large intestine, thus making the pup have to eliminate and defecate even more often than the larger-breed puppies. Nonetheless, puppies of all breeds have to "go" more often than they will as adults. This is due to their high metabolism, and it can also be due to their diet. Their high metabolism allows pups to maintain high bursts of activity for short periods of time. They burn calories at a faster rate than adult dogs and thus require a higher-caloric diet. A good-quality diet will allow the pup to digest more of his food, and good digestion means fewer, smaller and firmer bowel movements.

Another reason a pup might have to relieve himself more than an older dog is due to activity level. Puppies four months and older are very active. More activity increases the pup's need to eliminate. The movement loosens the urinary tract and the sphincter muscles while the pup is burning calories. As the calories burn, waste is produced. The more waste produced, the more the need for the pup to evacuate the waste.

WHEN HE NEEDS TO GO
There are particular times when a puppy will have to relieve himself.

Waking up from a nap means it's time to go out—quickly!

Regarding naps, a puppy can and will fall asleep anywhere.

Patty

Being aware of these times will help avoid accidents and improve the chances for expedient house-training. Always take your pup out at the following times:

1. After sleeping/napping. Pups automatically control their bladders while sleeping. Upon waking, they need the opportunity to relieve themselves. The smaller and/or younger the pup, the faster he will need access to his appropriate relief area.

2. After/during play. As mentioned, activity burns calories and thus produces waste. Activity also loosens the sphincter muscles. It is common for pups to eliminate while playing.

3. After/during training. Again, the activity burns calories and

produces waste. Often, a pup is rewarded with food treats while training. The treats may also increase the pup's need for water. The more water ingested, the greater the need to eliminate.

4. After meals. A puppy between two and three months of age will need to relieve himself within 15 to 20 minutes after eating. A pup 4 to 6 months of age will need to relieve himself within 30 to 45 minutes after eating.

SETTING A ROUTINE
The most expedient method of house-training your pup is to learn his schedule and then set up a routine that integrates your lifestyle and his needs. Rarely do busy puppy owners have the

opportunity to remain at home at all times. We have work, daily errands, children's schedules and many other activities. We can't sit and watch our pups all day.

When setting up a realistic daily schedule for your pup, you must consider your own schedule while, of course, incorporating your pup's needs. Puppies need to relieve themselves quite often throughout the day. If you work long hours away from home, you should hire a dog-walking service or ask a family member or neighbor to let your pup outside while you're gone. Without this help, it will take far longer to house-train your puppy, causing no end of frustration.

Crate training helps in myriad ways. First of all, it gives your pup a place where he can feel safe and secure. Canines appreciate the den-like atmosphere. They also instinctively rarely relieve themselves where they sleep, so the crate helps a pup learn control. Placing your pup in his crate will teach him how to control himself and quickly learn to "hold it" until he can go to his designated relief area. Paper training should not be an option unless you intend to allow this throughout the dog's life. Keep in mind that many dogs that relieve themselves on papers might also tend to do so in other parts of the house.

You should never leave your

Your pup will learn where he should "go" by being brought there on a leash each time a family member takes him out to potty.

adult dog in his crate during the day for more than five or six hours at a time, even less for a puppy. This would not be humane. Growing puppies need to stretch and exercise in order to develop proper muscles and strong bones, as well as to maintain their sanity. The wackiest, most out-of-control dogs are those that are cooped up for long periods of time every day. If you are considering getting a puppy or have already done so, do yourselves a favor and solicit some help.

In order to teach your pup where you want him to relieve himself, you'll need to go there with him, showing him the proper place, remaining there until he goes and rewarding him as soon as he does. This procedure is paired with teaching the pup to relieve himself on command.

The process is simple. Take your pup to the desired area on a loose leash. Once there, repeat his "potty word," such as "Hurry up," "Potty," "Business" or whatever you choose, until he goes. As soon as he goes, praise and reward him. Within a week or so, your pup will potty on command.

The following illustrates a sample schedule for the full-time worker:

Get up between 5 and 6 a.m., let your puppy out of his crate and take him outside. Remain outside with him and reward him immediately as he finishes his business. If

you wish to sleep longer, put your pup back in his crate as you go back to bed. If it's time to get ready for work, feed your pup and allow yourself ten minutes to start getting ready. If you hear your pup whining, take him outside immediately. That's his way of letting you know it's time to go. If you find that he has an accident before the end of the ten-minute period, begin taking him out directly after he eats.

After returning indoors, allow your pup to play in a pen while you eat breakfast and prepare for work. The pen should be set up in a safe place where your puppy can have space to play, yet not get into trouble. You cannot watch your pup while you're showering, shaving and cooking. If he's not being watched, he can get into trouble. You have to think of your pup as you would a human toddler. He should never be left unsupervised.

Prior to leaving the house, take your pup outside again, using the "potty word" until he does something. Upon going back inside, lure your pup into his crate, using a special treat such as a biscuit. Make sure the pup has some toys in the crate and plenty of water. Never leave your pup alone without access to water. If he loves to play in the water dish, consider a water bottle or a metal pail that clips to the side of the crate.

If you cannot come home every four hours, have your helper come to your house every four hours

Training, traveling and safety are a few of the uses of a sturdy crate, one of the most helpful tools for dog owners.

Unfortunately, your pup can't clean up his own accidents, even if he tries!

while you're gone. This is the maximum time that you should make your young puppy wait to stretch his legs and have a chance to relieve himself. You should also have your helper feed him midday, as puppies should be fed at least three times per day to aid in proper nutritional intake and digestion. Once he's over four months of age, he should be able to "hold" it for six hours, but he still shouldn't have to live day and night in a crate. If this is the case, you should not consider dog ownership. There are other types of pet that can withstand these long hours alone without undue suffering. Dogs are very social and don't fare well under these conditions.

Be sure to educate your helper by explaining how you are teaching your pup to potty on command and where you would prefer that

puppy relieves himself. Consistency is the key to reliability and, if everyone who handles your pup is consistent, the house-training process will take less time.

As soon as you return home at the end of the work day, let your pup outside and play with him. He's been cooped up for a good part of the day and needs to run. Once your pup reaches four months of age and has all of his vaccines, you can opt to take him to doggie daycare, where he can learn social skills and get lots of exercise while you are at work. Until then, you will need to give him as much exercise as possible. This means that the entire evening should be spent letting him outdoors, playing with him and working with him. Don't forget his evening feeding as well!

While you are home with your pup, let him outside every hour to hour and a half. The larger the breed, the longer the timespan. Remember, a toy-breed pup has a very quick metabolism and small bladder, thereby having to relieve himself more often.

At 10:30 to 11 p.m., make your last outdoor run. Make certain that your pup does his business. He'll have to hold it for six to seven hours overnight and should be allowed some comfort.

If, at any time, your pup does not do his business when you take him to his relief area, and you've waited a good ten minutes, you'll have to bring him back indoors and put him into his crate for a half-hour. Allowing him to remain loose is just setting yourself up for disaster, especially if you aren't watching him.

Having someone at home all day is, of course, the ideal scenario for housebreaking your pup. It's also best for normal physical growth and expedient positive-behavior formation. However, in our busy society this is more the exception than the norm. Here's a sample schedule for a stay-at-home puppy parent:

Between 5 and 6 a.m., let puppy outside. As soon as he relieves himself, let him play for a few minutes to stretch his legs. Around 6:30 a.m., give his morning meal. Go back outside around 6:45 a.m. Continue to take your pup outside throughout the day about every one to two hours, depending on how often he needs to go. You'll know by the amount of times he has accidents between your outdoor excursions. As a general rule, contain your pup in a pen or crate if you can't watch him. Let him out after/during play, after naps and directly after meals. If you have begun basic obedience training, take him outside or remain outside after completion of a training session.

Around noon, feed puppy his midday meal, then take him outside around 12:15. Again, take him out every hour or so, and then, between 4:30 and 5 p.m., feed his evening meal. Fifteen minutes later, take him outside.

The breeder raises the litter in an area that is easy to clean, often using newspaper or some other absorbent disposable material.

Newspapers are helpful in the beginning stages of house-training, unless puppy decides it's more of a toy than a toilet.

You do not need to give your pup his dinner when you and your family eat. In fact, you might want to feed him before you sit down to eat. This will allow you to make sure that he eats properly, and you will be able to then take him outside right away. He will also be full and sleepy when you sit down to eat dinner, making it less likely that he'll bother you while you eat. Take your pup out as needed during the evening/night hours, and don't forget the important last potty trip of the day before bedtime.

The aforementioned schedules are merely examples. Of course, many people do not work "nine-to-five," and even more people cannot be home all day. You will need to take a look at your lifestyle and personal schedule to produce something that works for you and your pup. Remember my saying that consistency is the key to reliability? Just because your life is inconsistent does not mean that you have to pass that on to your pup. Dogs are creatures of habit. Knowing what is going to happen and when will maintain your dog's sanity, preventing future behavioral problems. Try to find a happy medium. Most likely there are activities that engage your time during the day. At these times, your pup should be contained until you are able to keep an eye on him. Stick to the same feeding and potty schedule. You can do his obedience training at any time during the day, as training sessions take only five minutes at a time.

Did I mention that a long night's sleep is not an option?

Well, it isn't. Puppies, like babies, need to relieve themselves often and can only "hold it" for so long overnight. If your puppy cries during the night or early in the morning, needing to go out, don't take your time getting there. Jump out of bed and get him outside as soon as possible. Reward him as enthusiastically for going out in the middle of the night as you would during the day. Not only will this prevent accidents in his crate (and the mess you'll see in the morning after your puppy has walked in it), it also will help him associate his vocal outburst with the action of being taken outside, which is the beginning of his communicating to you when your puppy needs to relieve himself.

RECOGNIZE THE SIGNS

There are also visual cues that let you know when it's time to head outside. Your pup's sniffing the floor and turning in circles are clear signals that he is searching out a place to urinate. Sitting at your feet and whining is another signal. Going to the door, and even scratching at the door, is about as clear as he can be! Barking at you shouldn't be mistaken for "let's play" unless your pup just went outside to do his business a few minutes earlier.

Scent attraction is the basis of house-training, as puppy will follow his nose to find a pleasing relief site and use his sense of smell to locate the spot again and again.

However, if you need an unmistakable signal from your puppy that it's time to get outside, teach him to ring a bell or buzzer. With consistency (there's that word again), your puppy can learn to do this within a week. Begin by choosing one door in particular that you wish to use as the exit door to take your puppy to his relief area. This door should be in the area of the house where you and your pup spend the most time.

Hang a bell from the door-knob or place a buzzer near the door. Buzzers are now commercially available in pet shops. They are in the shape of a big paw print and deliver a sound when the paw print is pressed. A cow bell or huge jingle bell can be purchased at a craft-supply store along with a sturdy cord on which to dangle it from the doorknob. If your pup might have the tendency to scratch at the wall or door, you might want to install a planter holder to hold the cord and bell away from the wall.

Each time you take your puppy to the door to go outside, rub a small bit of cheese on the bell. When your puppy licks at the cheese, he will make the bell move, thus making it ring. As soon as the bell makes noise, take your pup outside to his relief area. While there, use your special "potty" word until your puppy does his business, there-upon praising and rewarding him for a job well done.

If you are using a buzzer mechanism, you will need to lure your puppy over the buzzer, using either a piece of food or a favorite toy. As soon as his foot presses on the buzzer, reward him with the lure and take him outside to his relief area.

Until your puppy starts going to the bell/buzzer on his own, continue to lure him there with the reward prior to going outside. Remember, you must do this every time you go outside; otherwise, your puppy won't associate the sounds with the situation.

Now you know how to set yourself up for success with house-training. But what happens when accidents occur? Is your puppy aware of what he is doing? Does he remember an accident he had an hour earlier? Can he be expected to hold it long enough for you to get dressed in the morning?

When a puppy has to urinate or defecate, it has to be done quickly. A puppy's sphincter muscles aren't yet fully developed, nor is his ability to know the house rules. Puppies don't learn through osmosis, nor can they read your mind. They must be taught.

Dogs have very good memories. They can remember something that occurred while very young even when they grow old.

They remember smells and places. They remember people and other animals. They even remember where they've relieved themselves. However, a puppy cannot know that it is wrong to potty in the house unless taught. That is up to you. It's unfair to punish a puppy for something that he doesn't know.

Watching your pup and letting him out at regularly scheduled times will teach him where to relieve himself. Rubbing his nose in the mess, yelling at him, hitting him and shoving him will only teach him to be frightened of you, not that he mustn't go potty in the house. There's a joke I once heard:

"How's Spike's house-training coming?" asks Fred's neighbor, Bob.

"Real good," answers Fred. "He goes outside on his own now. In just three days!"

"How'd you do that so soon?" asks Bob.

"After coming home from work three days ago, I saw a big pile in the living room and quickly grabbed Spike, dragged him over to it, rubbed his nose in it and threw him outside. The next day I came home from work and saw another big pile in the living room. Again, I grabbed Spike, rubbed his nose in it and threw him outside. Yesterday, when I came home, Spike ran into the living room, rubbed his nose in the still-steaming pile and rushed through the door as I came inside."

For those without a yard, their dogs can be trained to do their business while out for walks. Don't forget to clean up!

Fred puffs out his chest with pride. "What a dog!"

It is up to you to make sure your puppy learns in a positive manner, not only so he wants to perform the things you teach, but also so he learns the right things.

Your new puppy will be on his way to becoming a rewarding companion and family member when you learn to speak each other's language.

THINK DOG: WOOF, WOOF, GRRR, WOOF! YIP!

I don't expect you to be able to translate that. How can you when you can't see the entire picture? There's so much more to canine communication than sounds. Dogs communicate with their bodies, scent glands, sense of smell and sense of touch. Verbalizations come into play, but they are merely a minor part.

Most people believe that if they speak slower and louder, the puppy will understand their words. How can the pup understand anything? He doesn't speak English! How long would it take you to learn a foreign language? Months? Years?

Puppies do learn quickly, but mostly through your actions. As he learns your actions and your reactions to his specific behaviors, he will learn the words that go with those actions. Unfortunately, if you become frustrated, angry and ready to give up, your pup could respond with fear, aggression or total shutdown. How would you feel if you couldn't communicate with those around you?

Why do so many dogs end up at shelters and abandoned? Because the dog owners never took the time

**Always supervise
time spent
between children
and your puppy.**

to "think dog." To be an effective dog owner and trainer, you must first understand how dogs communicate. Once you can "think dog," you're well on your way to having the perfect canine companion.

Dogs are honest. They don't lie. They don't change their minds in the middle of something. They also don't understand any gray areas such as "sometimes," "maybe" and "it's okay this time but not next time." They don't understand the difference between your being dressed for work, for a night out or for playtime. All they know is how to gain food and attention. If something a dog does gains him a bite to eat or a touch from you, he will continue to do it because the action was rewarded.

Whatever you do, reward only those actions that you want your pup to do. For example, if you don't want a dog that jumps on you, don't give your puppy attention when he jumps on you. If you want your pup to play with his toys and not the chair leg, reward him when he plays with his toys by playing with him and praising him.

As humans, there is not much that we can do to control our scent emissions. We do inadvertently emit scents, depending on our moods, which is why our dogs are

Puppies are furry bundles of love and companionship, with a future as their owners' best friends! Author Miriam Fields-Babineau snuggles with a pair of Golden pups.

so quick to pick up on whether we're happy, sad, playful or angry. We can, however, control our body language and our words. It's how we use senses and signals that will determine our success in communicating with our puppy. Patience and persistence will bear fruit. Let's examine the senses and signals more closely, one at a time.

COMMUNICATING WITH YOUR DOG

VOICE

Your puppy doesn't come into your home knowing your language. Just as a human baby can learn any dialect, depending on the native language in his area, your puppy will learn the "dialect" at your home. But he must be taught. He must learn in a clear, consistent manner. The more you repeat something while pairing it with an object or action, the faster he will learn the word. This means that the more often you practice, the faster he learns.

Dogs learn best through your tone of voice. Dogs have three distinct tones to their own verbal communication: a high, happy tone, a demanding tone and a low, aggressive, threatening tone. Your using these tones at the appropriate times and with corresponding visual cues will teach your puppy

Australian Shepherds are bright and alert. You want this type of attentive look on your pup's face when you speak to him.

By using a treat to guide him, you show your puppy what you expect from him so that you can reward him for being a good dog.

the meanings of the words used with them.

When praising your puppy, use a high, happy tone of voice. Use a simple word such as "Good" or "Yes." Don't have a long conversation, explaining why the puppy is good. Just repeat the simple word with the enthusiastic tone. A human baby's first word might be "Da" or "Ma," not "Mommy, I want my bottle." Puppies learn best with simple, single words.

When giving your puppy a command, always precede it with his name. This will quickly teach him his name. Then, give the command with authority (the demanding tone). You don't need to

be loud, for your puppy can hear at least twice as well as you can. Just use your normal volume and demand the action from your puppy. He will listen far more quickly to your demand than to your question or plea. It's all in the tone you use.

When giving a command, say it only once. This will give your puppy a better idea of the meaning. If he doesn't do what you requested, and he most likely won't because he has no idea what you're saying, show him the action associated with the word. This can be done by either luring him into position with a treat or toy or gently placing him into position. Saying

Your puppy doesn't know what your words mean until you show him. Guidance and positive reinforcement help your pup learn to associate a behavior with your command.

the word once and reinforcing it with the action will teach your puppy the meaning of the word and to respond on one command. Some may think it better to repeat the command, because maybe the puppy didn't hear it. Or maybe if he hears it enough, he'll end up doing it by accident. This is not the way to teach your puppy. It will only cause confusion. If you wish for your puppy to respond to your

Pups respond to you and act accordingly. If your tone of voice is very excited, puppy will be excited, too!

first command, use only one command as you show him the meaning.

When correcting your puppy, use a low, growly tone of voice. This also does not need to be loud. When dogs growl at each other, it is actually fairly soft and menacing. It's a scary rumble in the throat. Your puppy will immediately respond to that sound. He'll remember it from his mommy and siblings.

Again, think of yourself in a foreign country. You don't speak the language and you are trying to find a place to sleep and eat. You try speaking to people, but they don't understand you. If you start shouting, they will shout back. But if you point to something and say the word, then the recognition kicks in. You explained your word. They

Coming to you must always result in something positive for the dog so that he never hesitates to respond to your call.

respond by using their own word for it and helping you attain what you want. Both you and the other person just learned something.

Now think of your hosting a guest from another country. This guest doesn't speak your language. You think that you're going to do a great thing and teach this person the names of things by pointing to them and saying the names over and over. Well, eventually your guest catches on. He now asks to eat by saying, "Go, go, go, table, table, table, sit, sit, sit, sit, sit." Kind of funny, huh? Yet your guest believes that this is the correct way to say, "Let's go to the table and sit for dinner." He doesn't see the humor in it.

VISUAL/BODY LANGUAGE

Dogs use visual communication more than any other mode. From the tips of their ears to the tips of their tails, every part of their bodies is used to transmit messages. Understanding the meanings of a dog's body language is the key to being successful in training and ultimately in establishing a long-term relationship with your dog.

Ears: The ears pricked forward mean that the puppy has been alerted. The alert stance can be a form of dominance or just an interest in something. If you are dealing with a young puppy, it is most likely the latter. If you are in the process of training your puppy, you can be sure that he will be

A Bull Terrier in an alert posture with ears held open to the sides.

The way this pup is holding his ears means that he is relaxed while being brushed with a grooming glove.

distracted frequently by things that grab his attention.

The ears held with their openings at the sides mean that the dog is paying attention or might even be wary of something. While involved in a training session, you will see his ears perking forward and moving to the sides. When he begins looking away from you, his attention span is gone. When dealing with a young pup, this can happen anywhere from 5 to 15 minutes into the training session.

When his ears are held lazily at the side, this means that the dog is relaxed. For canines with folded or hanging ears, look at the base. If it is facing forward, the dog is alert; if facing to the side, he is relaxed; if facing downward, frightened; if facing backward, worried. A relaxed puppy will not be able to concentrate on training. Young puppies require a lot of sleep. You'd be most successful doing the training session after his nap or before his meal.

The ears held slightly back may mean that the puppy is listening or might mean a slight form of submission. Often it is one and the same. The puppy is submissive to you and paying attention to your requests.

The ears held flat to the head most definitely mean submission and/or fear. A fear biter will hold

Eye contact (or lack thereof) measures a pup's level of dominance or submission.

his ears flat to his head. Do not force this pup to work. Coax him. Use food or toys to convince him that the training and interaction can be fun. Use caution and go slowly. Forcing this pup to work will only bring frustration and anger.

Head: A head held high means interest or being alert to a stimulus. It can also depict a dominant personality. With young pups, a high head means the puppy is having a good time and is interested in an activity. Many puppies like to present toys. A pup may pick up a toy and bring it to a littermate or to you, wagging his head and tail to instigate a game.

A head held at a relaxed angle—not high or low—is, of course, a relaxed dog. This may not be the appropriate time for a training session, but it is a great time to

get some household chores done.

The head held with the eyes pointing down shows a submissive dog. Your puppy is feeling sad or a little scared. Invite him into a game to make him feel better. However, if this is the visual cue given when he's been bad, then you know that whatever punishment you gave him was effective.

When the dog holds his head low and stretches his neck forward, this is depicting a very submissive greeting gesture, common in puppies and submissive dogs. Allow this pup to come to you. He is expressing sorrow, intimidation or fright. Don't go to him or he might roll over and submissively urinate.

Eyes: The eyes say a lot. Direct eye contact is a dominant gesture. If you meet a puppy that stares

Look at the base of this Dachshund's ears. They are facing forward, with his head held still, showing his alertness.

directly into your eyes without looking away, steer clear of taking him home. This is a very dominant animal. A dog should always look away first. Puppies, in particular, are submissive. If a pup doesn't look away, it can mean he's had minimal socialization with other canines or he is genetically dominant.

Blinking eyes are a form of submission. If you look directly into your pup's eyes and he blinks, he is showing you submission. Staring, then looking away, is acceptance. A pup may look at you for a moment and then turn away. There is no challenge there. He's accepted you. Looking with a soft facial expression, but not directly into your eyes, is a dog who is paying attention to you. He'll blink occasionally, but not constantly. He is relaxed. This pup is paying attention and not challenging your authority in any manner.

Mouth and Teeth: The mouth conveys a lot of information. Relaxed lips show a relaxed dog. Raised lips can mean aggression or submission. It depends on how the lips are raised. A single lip between the gum and teeth, showing just the tip of the incisor, is a sign of happiness and is especially cute. The lips raised in front, showing the front teeth only, is a sign of submission or fear, depending on the other visual cues. This might be associated with several other forms of body language, such as the tail wagging quickly, the head stretched forward and the dog either prancing around or standing still by his person. If the lips are raised and showing all the teeth, way into the back, that's an aggressive response, especially if the dog is growling in a low tone.

The tone of vocal emission has a lot to do with the dog's expressions. A high tone, such as a yip, is happy. A medium tone, such as a loud bark, is demanding. A low tone, such as a growl, is aggressive. Should your pup show his front teeth and yip, he is inviting you into a game. Showing the front teeth and barking at you is demanding you join his game. Showing all of his teeth and growling is a warning to stay away. It is rare to see a puppy with the latter expression, as most pups are still very submissive and easily impressed until the age of four to five months.

Body: A dog that is dominant will try to make himself look large. He'll be raised high on his toes, head held high, tail straight out and partly upward and hair along his spine raised. This is also seen in playful puppies. The body isn't really showing dominance at an early age, only pretending during play.

A relaxed dog will remain his normal size, and his tail will be held low (or, in the case of a dog with a tail that curls over his back, relaxed into position). His ears may swivel from side to side, but not perk forward. This pup is happy with his "station." He doesn't challenge anyone and accepts his siblings and pack members without contention.

A puppy that is concentrating and/or working will have a grin on his face. Yes, it's an actual smile, often seen while a puppy is enjoying his training time. He'll prance, his tail will wag slowly and his eyes will watch with a cheerful, bright expression.

A puppy that is inviting you to play will go down on his front end while leaving his hind end in the air, tail wagging. Some puppies will bark, demanding your participation in the game. Many people mistake this for aggression, especially if the puppy nips. This is puppy play in its purest form. Your puppy simply thinks that you need to join his game.

There are two different types of submissive behavior: active and passive. An actively submissive puppy is the type that might fear-bite if cornered and he sees no way out. He will hold his body low to the ground, hackles raised, neck stretched out and teeth bared. His tail will be between his legs. Never approach a puppy that shows these

Belly up! Lying on his back with his belly exposed, this dog is demonstrating a submissive posture.

behaviors. Some do not growl a warning, they simply lash out. If you insist that this is a puppy you want, approach very slowly, crouched down, and do not corner him. Take the time to allow the puppy to come to you. Do not reach out to pet him. Let the pup sniff you first. Everything must be taken very slowly and methodically. Allow your puppy to make the first move.

A passive-submissive puppy will try to make himself as small as possible. He will tuck his tail under his belly, lower his head and might roll over onto his back, showing you his belly. Some pups will urinate. Submissive urination should never be misconstrued as a house-training problem, and the puppy should never be punished for this type of accident. He is

This pup's body language reads submissive yet adaptable.

simply showing you that you are the boss and he defers to that position. Most puppies outgrow this behavior as they learn about their environment and new family pack.

TOUCH

Who doesn't want to hold and cuddle a puppy? Certainly not me! I find that the most therapeutic thing I can do is to cuddle with a puppy or kitten. Their warm little bodies and fresh odors, including the milk breath, are just terrific! It settles the soul and clears the mind.

Just as you love to touch your puppy, puppies love being touched, too. Every time you touch your pup, you're rewarding him. This means that if your puppy does something he shouldn't, you should not pick him up and scold him. You will only be rewarding him while correcting him, causing confusion. Plus, your pup won't like being picked up anymore.

Whenever pup does something of which you approve, touch him. Rub his head, ears or tummy. Scratch his back. As you cuddle with him, touch his feet, knead his ears, lift his lips. Do these things so that he will never be frightened of being touched all over, which will be helpful when you need to clean his ears, brush his teeth, clip his nails, etc.

TASTE

Besides touch and praise, taste is your pup's driving force. He will

Although a normal puppy behavior, nipping should never be tolerated, as it can escalate into biting as the dog grows up.

always be testing objects for edibility. Hmm, does this chair leg taste good? How about this finger? Maybe that plant is extra-juicy. His bite may not be hard and/or damaging while your pup is young, but it will get worse with age if the behavior is allowed to continue. Further, your pup could injure himself or make himself sick if he ingests harmful and/or toxic items. It is up to you to guide your puppy into tasting the right things, for his safety and the safety of your belongings.

Using food rewards during training will help promote your pup's enjoyment of the lesson and guide him in the right direction. It will also gradually increase his attention span, especially if you hold the training session before his regular meal. A hungry pup is an attentive pup.

Since your puppy will be getting treats during training before his meals, you'll want to be sure that you don't fill him up on "puppy candy," thus replacing his proper nutrition. Using pieces of his normal kibble as rewards, or natural treats such as freeze-dried liver in very small pieces, is helpful. You can also use little bits of vegetables or fruit, such as carrots, broccoli, apples or pears. These fresh foods are helpful in aiding his digestion prior to eating the processed kibble. Raw fruits and vegetables get his enzymes working, allowing for greater digestion of his meal.

You can use your pup's sense of taste to redirect him from chewing on the wrong things to playing with the right ones. Putting a horrible-tasting liquid (available in pet shops and made expressly to deter chewing) on the furniture and moldings in your home will help teach puppy to stay away from them. Giving him plenty of tasty safe toys will maintain his attention on the right things.

LESSONS FOR PUPPY

Everything you do with your puppy should be positive. Training is no different. Should you want your pup to do what you ask and look forward to working for you, he must have fun while he is performing. Play-training is the best means of ensuring that your puppy will love his training sessions. Keeping the lessons short is another way to make sure that your pup looks forward to his work.

Puppies have very short attention spans; generally about five to ten minutes. You will be most successful if you work with your pup for only five minutes at a time, but many times through the day. There are many ways that this method can fit into a busy schedule. It's far easier than trying to find a full half hour in your day to hold a training session.

You can train your pup for a few minutes prior to each of his meals. You can train him with other family members when they get home from work or school. You can also have a quick lesson whenever your pup has a burst of extra energy. Training him while he's alert and energetic is a great way to guide him into correct behavior instead of leaving him to invent his own activities, which, more often than not, are not things that you want him to be doing.

Puppy thinks his training time is play, when in actuality he is learning. Play-training is the most positive means of obtaining fast results that last a lifetime. A puppy that's having fun will maintain a longer attention span and look forward to each training session.

This Westie pup is targeting on the moving hand.

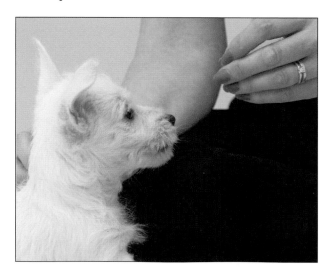

The way to a puppy's heart...

Begin each five-minute training session by having your pup "target." This focuses his attention and prepares him for learning new behaviors. In fact, he'll easily learn how to sit within the first few minutes of the targeting exercise. Many pups that might have dominant tendencies will still respond well to target training. It is also important to note here that any off-leash sessions should be done indoors or in a safely fenced or enclosed area only.

TARGET AND SIT
Begin this first training session by giving your pup a treat and saying "Good" as he takes it from you. Do this several times. Next, hold the treat in your fingers,

place your hand within his reach and wait for him to touch your hand with his nose. Say "Good pup!" (please substitute his name wherever I use "pup") and give him the treat. Repeat this two or three times.

In teaching the sit, moving the treat above the pup's head will make him look up while his rear goes down.

The pup may get
a little fidgety as
he tries to get to
the treat.

Next, move your hand a little to the left and then to the right. As your puppy keeps his nose on target, praise him and give him his treat. Add an up-and-down motion. Each time your puppy follows the target, reward him. Keep adding more and more criteria (movements) prior to each reward.

Now we'll work on the sit. (We still have a few minutes left in this first training session.) Place your targeting hand in front of pup's nose and lift it slightly upward toward his eyes. As you do this, say "Pup, sit." Your puppy will be watching his target and, as his head moves upward, his rear end will go down, like a see-saw. The moment his rear end touches the ground, praise him

Don't give puppy his reward until he performs the exercise correctly; otherwise, how will he learn?

and give him his reward. Make sure your timing is accurate. Puppies can get up just as quickly as they sit, so you want to be sure

Whether using a clicker or a treat lure, hold your target hand above the pup's head to coax him into the sit position.

Pup will follow the target, especially when it's a tasty one.

Put the targeting hand under pup's nose as you say "Come" to lure him to you.

Outdoor practice holds more distractions, so you will rely on your bait to keep pup's attention. When practicing outdoors, the pup should always be on lead if not in a fenced-in area.

your pup understands that he is receiving his reward for sitting. Thus, make sure he is in fact sitting when you give the treat!

Through this exercise, you are teaching your puppy to stop whatever he is doing, remain still and pay attention. This is very important, for your pup can't learn if you do not first obtain his interest. It takes far longer to explain how to do this than it takes to actually do it! Within your puppy's first training session, he should be able to target and sit as well as do the next exercise: come and sit.

COME AND SIT
One of the most important things your puppy can ever do is to come to you reliably when called. Young pups usually stick close to their pack members, so this exercise should come naturally. Puppies are very insecure until

reaching the age of four to five months. Your pup wants to be near you at all times.

Put your targeting hand under your pup's nose. Let him smell the treat and then step backwards two or three steps as you say "Pup, come" in a happy tone of voice. He'll immediately follow his target. Praise him enthusiastically as he comes toward you. If using a clicker, click the second he looks at you and give him a treat (appropriate times to click are shown in parentheses). Next, make him take a few steps toward you (click and give the treat). Build on his positive behavior in gradual increments. Don't expect the finished product right away.

When you stop moving backward, bring your hand over his head to an area just between his

After the puppy comes to you, lure him into the sit.

eyes so that he must look upward. Be sure that your hand is not more than two inches from his nose or he'll likely jump up. While he's looking up, say "Pup, sit." As soon as his rear end goes down, praise him (click) and give him his treat.

Continually increase your steps backward as you practice the come command. This way, your pup will learn to come from increasingly longer distances. Always make him sit when he arrives. The last thing you want your pup to learn is to come and then leave, or to come and jump up. A come and sit maintains his attention on you and teaches him appropriate behavior patterns.

Once your puppy is reliably coming and sitting, attach a lightweight leash (anywhere from four to six feet in length) to his regular neck collar. Let him drag the

Moving backward while luring pup to come to you helps with his momentum.

This Dachshund pup sits attentively after coming to his owner, awaiting the next instruction.

leash while you work with him. This will allow your puppy to become acclimated to the feel of the leash without having it pulled or used in a manner that he does not understand. As you will not be holding the leash yet, be sure to be in your safe, enclosed area.

ROUND ROBIN

When puppy is able to come and sit, it's time to involve the entire family. First of all, everyone

Lure the pup to come to you as you gather up his leash.

must do the come and sit exercises with him individually so that he learns to listen to everyone. Then, two of you stand about six feet apart, facing each other. These are the positions for the Round Robin game. The Round Robin game is the fundamental means of teaching the puppy how to perform specific behaviors such as sit, stay, down and come.

This type of training also has many benefits. First of all, your puppy has a great time, thus maintaining a longer attention span. Secondly, he learns to work for everyone in the family, not just one person. Third, he will become very tired, needing several hours of rest afterward. A tired puppy stays out of trouble, thus giving you peace of mind for a while.

Begin by calling your puppy to come. As soon as he sits and receives his treat, the next person calls him. Your puppy will come to each of you in turn and sit, facing the person who called him. Go back and forth a few times, then increase the distance between you by taking one big step backward while the other person has puppy's attention. You can continue increasing the distance up to about 15 feet; more than that would be too much at first. Young pups tire easily and, when tired, will lose their attentiveness.

The proper heeling position is directly by your side.

Your puppy is small, so hold the treat down low enough to be near his face.

Should the pup become distracted during his travels between family members, the person who last called him should try to regain his attention by putting a treat under the pup's

The puppy should not jump up to get at the treat. The idea is to use the treat to keep him walking next to you.

nose. If this is not enough, then that person should take hold of the leash (remember that he should be dragging the leash at this time) and bring the puppy to him. This is very important, for your puppy will quickly figure out whose voice has meaning and whose does not. Puppies will not listen to those who do not back up their commands.

HEEL AND SIT

The Round Robin and the come and sit exercises will easily be transferred into working on the heel and sit. Pup already knows most of it. He knows to follow the target and that when he arrives at that target, he must sit to receive it. Thus, all you have to do is transfer your target to your left side instead of holding it in front of you. Pup will then go to your left side and sit.

Begin by having your puppy do a come and sit. As soon as he sits, place yourself at his right side, your left leg even with his shoulder. This is the proper heeling position. It is important that your puppy learns to remain in this position; otherwise, he cannot be properly attentive. You can either let the leash continue to drag or pick it up, hold it in your right hand and keep it very loose so that you don't pull against him.

Get puppy's attention by showing him the treat, then keep

As your pup gets older, you may find it beneficial to use a training collar, like the head collar, for formal leash work. A trainer can advise you about these collars and how to use them properly.

When you stop walking, the pup should be lured into the sit position. The heel begins and ends with the dog sitting by your side.

your target by your left leg at knee level. When his nose targets on your hand (click), offer the reward as you praise him. Once he's finished with his treat, say "Pup, heel" and take a step forward on your left leg. Moving your left leg first becomes puppy's visual cue for the heel command. He'll learn to move forward as your leg moves forward.

Go only one step and stop. Pup will most likely follow his target and move forward with you. As soon as he does, praise him (click). When you stop, say "Pup, sit." As soon as he sits, give him praise (click) and treat. Keep increasing the number of your steps each time you do the heel exercise. Within a short time, you and your puppy will be walking 5, then 10, then 20 steps and more. Once you get this far, you can begin incorporating turns. Do a turn and stop directly after the turn. This will keep puppy at your side. During later training, executing turns will be the best means of maintaining your pup's attention.

Do the heeling exercise only three times and then give your pup a break. This will maintain his attention and positive associations with the heel command. Within the five-minute training period, you can do a series of four or five mini-walks and several come-and-sits.

If, at any time, your puppy becomes disenchanted by his target and more interested in the leaves blowing by, place the reward under his nose and try drawing him closer to you. Decrease the amount of steps between your start and stop. Maybe his current reward isn't

As soon as the pup is even with your leg, lure him to sit, then treat or click.

Lure the pup around turns with the treat. He will follow the target hand as you change direction.

Pet your puppy
and give him
some time to
relax after
working with
him.

doesn't always have to be food. If your pup loves to chase a ball or stuffed toy, he will focus his attention on that item held in your hand.

Another thing you can do to maintain his interest once he's become rather good at heeling is to change your pace now and

Maintain the treat lure at pup's eye level as you walk so that he keeps moving with you.

attractive enough. Try something else. If he was interested in the leaves or a toy, maybe holding the object of his interest would maintain his attention. The reward

Encourage the puppy to keep pace with you, not lag behind, around turns.

The head halter is a useful training tool for dogs who pull on the lead, but is not necessary in the beginning stages of training.

then. Pup must learn to remain at your side whether you are walking slow or fast. In fact, one of the ways to obtain the attention of a distracted puppy is to jog a bit. Most puppies will eagerly run after a fast-moving playmate. Make any pace changes in short bursts. Always praise your pup as he catches up with you. As soon as he's even with your leg, stop,

A treat lure should coax pup to put his nose down, and hopefully his whole body will follow.

tell him to sit and reward him with praise (click) and his treat. Should he overshoot, turn to the right and lure him back to your side, again stopping and rewarding him when he sits.

DOWN

The next command on your puppy-training agenda is the down exercise. This is initially taught during the Round Robin game. It should be interspersed with the sit commands. In one round, your puppy sits and in the next round, he sits and then lies down before the next person calls him. This is very important, as you don't want the puppy to believe that he arrives and immediately lies down. He should always come and sit first, awaiting his next command. Dogs are easily pattern-trained. Should you repeat something as few as three times, puppy will learn the pattern and tend to anticipate your commands. While it's nice to know that your puppy really wants to please you that much, it doesn't mean he's obedience-trained, only pattern-trained.

The down can sometimes be difficult to teach because it is a submissive position. However, due to most young puppies' easily giving in to dominance, it shouldn't be an issue. Some pups might feel dominant at an early age and not take to going down

Practice the down command during the heel exercise with the pup at your side.

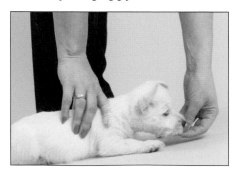

Gentle pressure on the shoulder blades while targeting helps pup attain the down position.

easily. Be certain to make teaching this exercise as positive as possible by using a treat or toy that is totally irresistible.

Once your pup has come and sat in front of you, put the reward beneath his nose and bring your lure and signal down to the floor as you say "Pup, down." He should follow the lure, at least with his nose. Even if he only looked at it, reward him for the gesture. Next time, ask for more of a response, such as moving his front end down. The time after that, he should put his front elbows all the way down and the time after that, he should touch all the way down to his tummy, tucking his haunches under. If your pup is resistant to putting his entire body all the way down, apply a little pressure just behind his shoulder blades as you show him the lure and give the down command.

When your puppy understands the down during the Round Robin game, you can add it to your heel and sit repertoire. Every two or three times that you stop, have your pup sit and then lie down prior to receiving his reward and going into the heel again. The more you practice this exercise and maintain

A puppy will surely flop down when it's time to rest, but he may be more resistant to comply with a command to assume the down position.

This French
Bulldog must be a
pro at the
sit/stay to pose
so politely.

In the beginning stages of teaching the stay, your target hand should be almost, but not actually, touching the pup's nose.

everything in a positive manner, the less your pup will think of the position as a vulnerable one and the more he will consider it a rewarding experience. After all, he gets treats and tummy rubs while lying down. What could be better?

STAY

The next command your pup should learn is the stay. This can be the most difficult thing for a puppy to do. Young pups are constantly in motion. Remaining still in the same spot is not at the top of a pup's list of favorite things. If you can train your pup to remain still for even 30 seconds of a sit/stay or down/stay, it will be quite an accomplishment. If you can work it up to a minute, your pup is a genius and you're a master trainer!

The stay command will need to be done through a gradual increase of your criteria, using successive approximation. This type of training is used whenever gradually increasing the criteria for any given exercise. For example, when you began teaching your pup to heel by taking one step and building on that, you used successive approximation. As he accomplished a couple of steps, you went on to more steps in between each stop and sit. Before long, you were walking ten steps and doing turns. You

When beginning to teach the sit/stay, hold the treat near the pup's nose, but do not give it to him until he has been in the sit position for three to five seconds. You will gradually increase the length of the sit before treating.

Stand in front of the pup, with the two of you facing each other, for the sit/stay.

One second equals one "Good boy." The first time you do a stay, you'll say "Good boy" one to two times. The next time your pup gets two to three "Good boys." And so on, until puppy can remain in place for at least 30 seconds.

By the time you reach five to six words of praise, puppy may start popping up and trying to go to the next person, who might be more willing to offer a treat for a simple sit. You can prevent this by stepping on his leash when he arrives and sits in front of you. Should he get up, you can easily

successively increased the criteria for each reward—the treat.

Begin teaching this exercise by first playing the Round Robin game. When your pup arrives and sits, place the palm of your hand in front of his nose, (not touching him) and say "Pup, stay." Hold the treat near his nose but don't give it to him for three to five seconds. Praise him as he remains in place (click). Give him his treat, and then the next person should call him to come. Each time you have the puppy come and sit, increase the amount of time that he has to maintain a stay before receiving his reward.

Since you'll have a lot to do within a short time frame, looking at your watch is not something you can coordinate. You can more easily count the seconds by using, "Good boys."

bring him back into position by luring him with the treat and repeating your stay command. After replacing him in approximately the same location, again tell him to stay, but this time shorten the amount of time to two or three "Good boys." Sometimes you need to regress in order to progress. When working with a puppy, everything needs to remain as positive as possible. Going back to a comfortable zone (in this case, less time in the stay) increases the pup's desire to perform.

Each time you have a training session, increase your pup's stay time. In a few weeks, he'll be able to remain in one spot without any problem. Practice the stay exercise with the down position as

well. Remember to vary all of the exercises in order to keep your puppy attentive and learning to listen to you rather than learning a pattern.

When your pup is able to remain in the sit/stay for upwards of 30 seconds, it is time to introduce the next variable—moving

The first step of the down/stay is getting the dog into the down position.

Once the pup is down, teach the stay with the same visual cue as you did for the sit/stay, with your palm in front of his face.

As you progress, you will move around the puppy as he holds the sit or down position.

around him as he remains sitting. This needs to be done with a gradual increase of movement. You begin by stepping side to side while you face your pup. Then, the next time you do a stay command, step on either side of him—from head to back legs on both sides. When your pup learns to remain sitting throughout your movements, you can begin doing a complete circle around him.

Always place your puppy back into the sit position every time he gets up. He must be replaced as close as possible to the original location where you told him to perform his sit/stay. This way, he learns to remain where you told him to stay, not where he chooses to stay. Even

being allowed to scoot into a position following your movements will decrease the possibility of your pup's learning to stay in one place. He must remain where you put him, facing the same direction. His head can follow your movements, but his body can't. This is a difficult concept to young puppies, but one that is important to learn.

As your pup accepts your walking around him, try doing so in both directions. Then begin to increase your distance as you move around him. Add a foot or two of space between you and your pup each time you do a sit/stay. Within a week or two, you should be able to get 6 feet away from him as he remains in his sit/stay.

Practice this exercise with the down/stay as well. The only difference will be that, instead of your stepping side-to-side in front of your pup, you'll begin your side-to-side movements along his right side and proceed to walk around by going around his back end first. While lying down, your pup is less likely to pop up if you go behind him, for he's not as attracted to your moving away from him as he is to your walking in front of him.

LEASH TRAINING
In nearly every society, there are leash laws for dogs being walked out in public. You'll need to keep

your puppy leashed while visiting the veterinarian or groomer, while walking in the park or while strolling through your neighborhood. Thus it is imperative to teach your pup how to behave while on a leash.

When your pup is young, use a lightweight cotton leash that is easily washable. The leash will be dragged through the dirt, urinated on, chewed on and played with, so you want one that will hold up to frequent laundering. Then again, you might want a couple of these leashes, one to use while the other is being washed, or one to use as backup when puppy destroys the other one. Hey, no puppy is perfect!

Up to this point, puppy has learned everything with the leash dragging behind him or while not wearing one. If he has been prepared for wearing a leash by dragging a leash while working, he'll be ready for formal leash training. If not, start putting it on and getting him used to it while he is working and playing. Practice all of his "puppy kindergarten" behaviors prior to doing anything on a leash. Continue to hold all training sessions for only five minutes at a time. Keep him wanting more. Even the leash work should only consist of five minutes at a time. This is especially important when puppy is learning new things. He will be more easily tired and stressed,

and thus you will lose his attention more quickly.

With leash training, you can begin by doing the come and sit

The trainer is giving the down/stay signal, but this pup has taken the command a little too far!

with the leash dragging. You want to continue to promote pup's off-leash behaviors while he's learning to work on a leash. You also want him to continue thinking of training as a game. Make sure you have lots of treats or his special toy handy to reward him at the appropriate times. If you have been using a clicker to bridge puppy's behaviors, you can either place it in your right hand with the leash or put it away, using the word "Good," "Yes" or "Yippee," or making a clicking noise in your cheek as a substitute. You will need both hands available for leash training. The left hand should hold the reward while the right hand holds the leash. Keep your right hand either on your left hip or at your belly.

The same rules apply whether heeling on or off leash. The treat should be held near your left calf; you should bait your pup the entire time and you should praise and reward with the same good timing. Nothing changes just because you're holding a leash.

You will need to take care that the puppy doesn't get the leash wrapped around his legs as you work. This is one of the hazards of using a loose leash. The alternative is to keep the leash tight, but then you might accidentally pull on his collar, causing the pup to back away from you and have a bad experience. It will take far more work to overcome a bad experi-

ence than to maintain consistent positive training sessions.

Since this is more of a formal training exercise than when you first introduced the heel, you will utilize more turns and stops to maintain the pup's attention. He may receive pressure on his collar from time to time, but you should never drag your pup. If he lags or shows interest in something else, always coax him with the bait under his nose and slap your leg while using an enthusiastic tone of voice.

When preparing to stop and sit, hold the leash firmly against yourself as you stop. Immediately show puppy his bait and lure him into a sit as you give the command. Bridge the action and reward him, then continue on. It would be a good idea not to touch him at this time, as this releases him from concentration and you will have to call him to you again to regain it. As soon as the pup sits and gets his reward, continue on with another round of heeling.

Each time you stop, don't forget to vary your exercises. Ask the pup to sit or down/stay as you move around him. You can also have him just sit and then continue on with the heel. Even though this is considered formal training, you must keep the sessions short. Your canine is still very young and has a short attention span and tolerance. Five minutes at a time is all he needs.

WHAT IS NORMAL?

All canines go through critical behavior periods that can heavily impact their future. This chapter discusses when they occur and how to handle them. Being aware that your pup is merely behaving in a normal manner and that he will soon outgrow certain annoying or otherwise unbalanced behaviors will help you through some tough times. You know how children go through the "terrible twos?" Or later on, as adolescents, how they become willful and tend not to listen? Puppies go through these phases, too. It's very natural for a pup that once followed you every-

where to suddenly want to go off on his own adventures.

Between the ages of one and four months, pups go through many behavioral changes. All of these changes can be grouped into two periods: socialization and ranking. After four months of age, there are several more behavioral periods, but since we are concentrating on young puppies in this book, I will only discuss the two you will need to understand at this time.

SOCIALIZATION: 3–12 WEEKS
The socialization period is the most important time in a puppy's life.

A pup's early socialization comes from interaction with his mom and littermates. Dinner for this Golden pack is truly a family affair.

When out for walks, dog-friendly people will surely want to meet your puppy. This gives you the opportunity to show people how to approach your pup and to observe pup's reactions to strangers.

His experiences at this age will foreshadow his entire life. The pup must receive proper instruction from his mother, then interact with his siblings and finally learn how to mingle with people and new animals.

Between three and seven weeks, a pup will be within his litter. He'll be learning how to interact with his mother and littermates. He's learning play and social skills. He's also learning social order, bite inhibition and coordination. Without these experiences, he will later develop behavioral disorders that will cause problems in his new home. A puppy should never be removed from his litter before the age of seven weeks. It won't hurt for people to visit and play with him and his littermates before this time, but he needs to remain with his canine pack to learn things that a human can't teach him.

It is also a good idea for puppies to be exposed to loud noises during their early lives. This will prevent fear reactions as they grow older. The sounds of things

like vacuums, sirens, construction vehicles and thunderstorms can be obtained on tape or CD and played a couple of times each day to desensitize the pups to these noises. Perhaps the breeder will have done this or something similar to acclimate the pups to a range of sounds.

Puppies generally go to their new homes between 7 and 12 weeks of age. It is at this time that the responsibility for the pups' learning falls entirely on the new owners. Your puppy will be going through his vaccinations, getting to know his family and environment and beginning his training. His behavior will be a direct result of your actions. For example, if he shows fear of an object or situation, do not coddle him. Coax him to

Introduce your puppy to the family cat carefully, in a controlled and supervised situation.

Not all dogs and pups enjoy sharing their toys with canine pals, so supervision is essential. If any problems arise, removing the toy should put everyone back on good terms.

Your puppy's experiences with children during the socialization period will impact his future attitude toward young people, so you want these meetings to go well.

investigate and reward him when he does so. Coddling can be anything from picking him up to speaking in a "cooing" tone of voice. This reaction will cause him to become more fearful. Try instead to put toys and treats near the object of his fear. Touch the object yourself, showing him that it's nothing to be afraid of.

Your young pup will need to be exposed to as many people and other types of animals as possible. You can let your pup socialize with other dogs, provided that he has received the necessary vaccinations and that the other dogs are healthy and up to date on their inoculations. It is most important to expose the pup to children and men, for these are the people that dogs tend to fear most: children because of their erratic movements and high-

pitched tones of voice and men because of their domineering presence and low tones of voice.

When you begin training, be sure to involve the entire family. Your pup is a clean slate right now, and he needs to learn to respond to everybody. It is far easier to begin training right away than to correct inappropriate behaviors later.

By three months of age, a pup has an adult dog's brain capacity. This means that he can learn both simple and complex concepts. You can teach him to come, sit and lie down, as well as teach him a couple of tricks and how to behave in the house. These lessons include what he can (his toys) and can't (the furniture) put his mouth on, where he needs to relieve himself (outdoors, preferably, or a specific location set up for him indoors) and how to respond to specific stimuli such as hand signals and verbal commands, the presence of other people and animals and loud noises.

Your puppy will be putting his mouth on everything. This is how he discovers and explores. It does not mean, however, that he should be allowed to do this on anything other than his toys. A natural behavior should not necessarily be an allowed behavior. It is up to you to guide him in the proper direction.

During this time, your puppy will follow you everywhere. He is very pack-oriented and will remain close. He'll seem to be already trained to come because he'll eagerly wish to be by your side. He won't get into much mischief, because he will tend to sleep a lot.

RANKING PERIOD: 12–16 WEEKS
At this age, a puppy is starting to teethe. His front teeth are falling out and new ones are coming in. Not only are his gums uncomfortable but he also seems to have far more energy than before. He can play for longer periods of time, and he sleeps for shorter periods. He puts his mouth on everything, especially his pack members, meaning your family.

His mouthing behavior is not entirely teething and play, as he is also discovering the pack hierarchy—namely, who's in charge. That's why this age is called the ranking period. Your pup will try your patience at all times. Unless you give him positive options to gain your attention, he'll come up with his own ways— which might not be so positive.

Puppy will begin to wander off. While he used to remain at your side when outdoors or in the house, now he takes off and doesn't listen to your beckoning. When he takes off indoors, he's likely to get into trouble. There are things to jump on and things to chew. There's a corner that nobody visits that's a great place to relieve himself. Outdoors, there are squirrels and leaves to chase and other people and dogs to visit. The world is wide open to adventure.

You will need to supervise your pup at all times, indoors and out. If you can't watch him, he will need to be contained in an area where he cannot hurt himself or get into trouble. You will also need to continue socializing him as much as possible. The one thing that will be most helpful in more ways than one is for him to play with other dogs. Not only will it wear him out and keep him out of trouble but he will also continue to receive those valuable social skills that he needs to grow into a mentally sound companion.

Always reinforce his positive behavior and redirect him from any negative behavior. Train him whenever you have the opportunity. His attention span will be increasing, but continue to keep his lessons short. Remember, five minutes at a time!

Socializing with well-behaved adult dogs is very important. Puppies learn social skills from other dogs, so you want puppy to have good role models.

No Bad Pups!

I've mentioned how puppy owners need to watch over their puppies with an eagle eye and how prevention is the best way to avoid unpleasantries. These two elements alone will steer your pup in the right direction. However, there are some puppies that have already learned undesirable behaviors. It will be your job to overcome them and avoid any other problems that might come along.

Most undesirable behavior has been promoted, albeit uninten-tionally, by visitors and by those who played with the litter prior to your bringing your puppy home. There's nothing more fun than to sit among a litter of puppies and have them climb all over you, bite your feet and fingers, jump on you and pull on your clothing. It takes only a few minutes for a puppy to realize that he is rewarded for these behaviors through attention and pleasant tones of voice.

When you bring your pup home, relatives and friends will

Introducing your new dog to friends and neighbors provides excellent socialization for your pet.

allow your pup to do things you don't want him to do. Inconsistency among family members is the most common problem, as one might want to roughhouse with pup while the other wishes to cuddle with pup and not get nipped in the process. Do you really want your puppy to think you're initiating a fun wrestling match every time you go to pet him? Have you ever heard the phrase "Education begins at home?" This pertains as much to puppies as it does to people. In fact, before the puppy even comes home, you and your whole family will need to sit down and have a long talk about how the new pup will be educated and the importance of everyone's being consistent.

If you are reading this book, then you understand the importance of first teaching yourself before you can train your puppy. You need to understand the basics of puppy ownership, how to communicate with your pup and how to maintain consistency. While teaching yourself at home, it is imperative that you pass this knowledge on to all who might be in contact with your puppy, especially family members.

The first thing that goes when a family is disrupted is the puppy. He will be the object of contention and, therefore, while seeking relief from this perceived irritation, many people opt to get rid of

Puppy needs his own safe area in the home, a "puppy-proofed" place where he can feel cozy and stay out of trouble.

the pup when problems arise. In reality, the pup was actually the only innocent one in the entire situation. How many people would get rid of their babies if they fought over diaper-changing and feeding routines? Is a puppy any more disposable because of disagreements over whose turn it is to walk him, feed him, take him out to potty? Hopefully, you got a puppy because you all really wanted canine companionship.

Regardless, a puppy is not disposable. It is your responsibility to raise him right; he can't do it on his own. It is also your responsibility to make sure that everyone in the family is consistent. Remember, there are no bad puppies, only inconsistent and

Pups love to be held and cuddled. Handling is an important part of forming a bond that will last for the dog's entire lifetime.

uninformed puppy owners. In case you're searching for a magic pill to cure all of your pup's behavior problems and to prevent any new ones, try the word "redirection." Now, just chanting the word over and over won't solve or prevent behavioral issues. You have to put it into practice! Be consistent with redirection and educate others to accept it as a way of life with your puppy.

I will address the most common behavioral issues in puppy raising, like jumping up, mouthing/biting, chewing, barking and chasing other family pets, and I will use redirection to cure every one of these problems. All of these behaviors are very natural to your

puppy's play routines. When pups play together, they bite each other, jump on each other, bark at each other and chase each other around. The only time they are corrected for these behaviors is when the play gets rough and a pup cries out in pain. If the pup causing the problem doesn't get the message and stop, his mother usually steps in and takes care of the issue. The formidable puppy won't easily find a playmate if he continues with socially unacceptable behavior, so he learns to back off when he hears the other pup yip or when the other pup moves away from him to avoid being hurt again.

Our best means of curing behavioral issues is to not allow

pups to think of people as play-mates in the first place, but to instead think of us as mother figures. Mother will put up with a bit of play but will quickly correct a pup for unacceptable behavior with a growl and pressure on the nose or neck. The correction behaviors used by a canine parent are similarly useful when used by a human parent. Granted, we really don't want to grab our pup with our teeth as we growl. This would give us hairballs! But we can use our hands to apply appropriate pressure as we use our voices to emulate a growl.

While this is a good means of curing an already-occurring problem, what about preventing the problem from occurring in the first place? Redirection. There's that word again. Take your pup's attention off the thing you don't want him to do and direct it onto something you do want him to do.

CURES TO COMMON PROBLEMS

THE JUMPING-BEAN SYNDROME
Your pup has learned to jump up because he's been rewarded for doing so. Initially, he may have done this to reach your nose for a proper canine greeting. He was given a reward of kind words and/or touch, so he now knows how to gain your attention.

There are several ways to cure this behavior. The method you use depends on the situation. Redirection is the most positive means of overcoming the jumping-bean syndrome. When your pup jumps up on you, step away and immediately lure him into a sit. As soon as he sits, praise him and give him his reward of attention. This will quickly teach the pup to sit for attention instead of jumping up for it. This also means that you must be aware of what your puppy is doing when he sits at your feet, looking at you. If you ignore him, he'll go back to jumping on you, because that's how the sit-for-attention game got started. If you reward him as soon as he sits, the jumping-bean syndrome will soon disappear. You always need to be observant of pup's actions.

Now, what happens when other family members don't practice redirection techniques? Maybe they are too young or they refuse to listen to your pleas for

It's fun to "get down" and play with dogs, but you can't literally let them walk all over you.

Jumping up is not the correct way for your puppy to greet someone.

them to be consistent. You cannot step in and redirect the pup as easily, especially when someone is entering the house or room and he wishes to greet the newcomer with enthusiasm. In this situation, you'll need to use a sharp noise to redirect the pup. The sharp noise will immediately take his mind off jumping. It will be up to you to redirect him into the sit, for the other person is unwilling to do so or doesn't know that he's supposed to. How many times have you heard, "Oh, he's just being friendly" or "It's

okay, I don't mind his jumping on me. It's cute." These people don't realize how they are perpetuating an undesirable behavior. They don't understand that the cute pup will grow into "monster dog," redesigning guests' clothing with pawprints, tears and punctures, possibly injuring people and even becoming the cause of your friends and relatives not wanting to come by very often.

I have found that the most effective noise is a can with pennies in it. The can should be made of tin or steel, not aluminum or plastic. You can use a small paint can or a coffee or tea tin. Place 15 pennies inside and seal the top so that it doesn't open when you shake the can. You may want to make three or four of these "no-jump boxes" and place them strategically around your home. The best places are the front door, family room, kitchen and back door.

When pup jumps up, shake the no-jump box in an up-and-down motion only once or twice as you growl "No!" As soon as pup stops jumping, crouch down to his level and lure him into a sit. This teaches him the appropriate response to hearing the sound. You don't want to frighten him with the no-jump box, but he should be wary of it. As you will soon discover, this will also help with other behavior-modification techniques.

MOUTHING/BITING/CHEWING

All puppies bite. If your pup bites, it doesn't mean that he is aggressive. Puppies use their mouths as we use our hands. They grab, pull, shake and taste. These are all common behaviors of any toddler, human and canine alike. It is through these behaviors that they learn how to interact with their environment. It is through your reactions and direction that they will learn the correct way to do this.

While it might be cute to have a puppy biting your arms and fingers, it is not appropriate behavior. As the pup matures, this type of play turns into dominance and the pup's jaws get stronger, which can be painful. A puppy's sharp teeth should be indication enough of what can happen later. Puppies have small sharp teeth for a reason. It is their means of ensuring survival until their jaws develop.

There is no such thing as an accidental bite. It was merely allowed in some form or another, whether you realize it or not. You must always be aware of what your pup puts his mouth on. Make sure that there are plenty of toys available and that you always supervise him. This will prevent your pup from ingesting anything dangerous, chewing electrical cords or putting his mouth on people.

When pup tries out the chair leg, you can either growl at him, shake your no-jump box to remove his attention from the wood or coax him into a game with one of his toys. The latter is the most positive means of stopping the behavior, but is also the most temporary. The puppy has to learn that the chair leg is not an acceptable chew toy. To learn this, he must receive a correction. The growling and/or rattle of the box will usually serve as enough of a deterrent. However, there are some stubborn pups that will look at their people as if to say "make me" and return to chewing the chair leg.

While redirection can often serve its purpose in curing mouthing/biting/chewing behaviors, it is not always 100% successful. In this case, you need to use canine communication. How does mother dog correct her pup? She takes the pup's muzzle or neck in her mouth, presses against him and growls.

How will we emulate that? Take the scruff of the pup's neck into your hands, look him in the face and growl. Then release him, show him one of his toys and invite him into a game with it. This method incorporates both canine communication and the human technique of redirection. This way, the pup isn't learning through trial and error as he would in a pack situation. You are showing him the road to good behavior, and you can use these behavior-modification techniques for mouthing, chewing and biting.

EXCESSIVE BARKING

While not a very prevalent behavior in pups, excessive barking can turn into an annoying behavior later. Most puppy barking is due to the pup's being involved in a fun game or trying to instigate a game. As the pup matures, barking will be a means of "talking back" when you scold him. Hey, you barked first!

Since most puppy barking is associated with play behavior, you shouldn't do anything to correct his barking, provided he is playing with his toys or with another pet. You can try giving him a toy to chew on, which will close his mouth for a little while, but if you expected a quiet pet, you should not have gotten a dog! Dogs are very lively creatures that love to interact with others. The best thing you can do is make sure that pup's verbalizations are used at the appropriate times, either during play or, when he is older, as a territorial alarm to alert you to anything out of the ordinary. In order to guide pup into proper barking habits, reward him when he barks at these times. Do not reward him for barking at inappropriate times; merely redirect him into another behavior.

CHASING CATS

If it moves, pup will chase it. That's part of being a predator. It is called the prey drive, and all dogs have it. Most cats will run from a predator. A small percentage will remain still, make themselves look bigger and threaten the predator. Either of these situations can prove dangerous to your puppy.

Cats have a high prey drive also. They also have great self-preservation instincts and the tools to go with them: claws and needle-sharp teeth. Unless you have a cat that was raised with dogs, there will be problems with integration of the two pets. A cat that is acclimated to the movements and actions of a canine will know that she shouldn't run away from the puppy and should generally accept the pup's overtures to a point. When that point is reached, the cat will bat at the pup with the claws retracted. The cat might hiss or spit at the pup. For most pups, this is enough of a hint that he went too far. For some, however, it's just an invitation to play harder.

For the bolder pup that learns things the hard way, a cat might prove very dangerous. You will need to step in and redirect your puppy into another game; otherwise, you are risking his being scratched by the cat. A means of redirecting the pup from a distance would be to spray water in his face. This distracts him from the cat game and might even teach him to associate the water spritz with incorrect behavior, thus curing the cat-chasing problem altogether.

Redirection can also be used for games of tag. Cats that have

Cats usually don't relish a puppy's overtures, and pups are usually rather persistent in trying to make friends.

been raised with dogs love to instigate these games. A cat will approach the dog, rub against the dog, flick her tail at the dog's nose and then run. The cat is asking the pup to chase her, and she loves to get the puppy in trouble for racing through the house after her. You remember the Garfield cartoons, don't you? Garfield loved to get the dog in trouble! The game is especially fun when the cat jumps onto a high perch and the pup can't follow her, and the pup instead jumps on the closest piece of furniture, leaping up and barking.

This game can be more than annoying to you. It causes a ruckus in the house as well as a mess. However, it's also quite entertaining—at least to the cat. There's really no means of preventing this from happening, but you can prepare for it by putting your pup on a leash and keeping him close by. When he is teased by the cat, redirect him to a toy and play with him. He is merely looking for interaction, and your attention will fulfill that need. If he's faster than you and has already responded to the cat, put your foot on the end of the leash and hold him there until you can redirect him onto something else. Meanwhile, spritz the cat with water to get her away from the puppy. Teaching your cat proper manners around the puppy would also be helpful, but that is another book altogether!

This pup is investigating a cat, but the cat would rather keep a distance between them.

THE WELL-ROUNDED PUP

Throughout this book you have observed some specific themes: all training should be done in a positive manner, your pup must be watched at all times and he needs as much socialization as possible. All of these matters are attended to through obedience training, constant observation and play with other animals and people. In order to have a well-rounded pup that will be enjoyed by all, don't take shortcuts or leave your pup to his own devices. Dogs can't read our minds. They learn through experience and they gain knowledge from others—us. They are creatures of habit and molded by their environment.

DISTRACTION-PROOFING

When you begin taking your puppy out in public, you want people to be awestruck by his good behavior. You want your veterinarian to be able to give him an exam without struggling. You want to let him play with other dogs, safe in the

When out on a walk with your pup, he will be alert and curious about everything.

Plenty of activity and structured playtime will keep your dog happily occupied.

knowledge that he will play nicely.

In order to accomplish these things, your pup will need distraction-proofing. This is very difficult for a young puppy, as everything presents a distraction, from a new person to blades of grass blowing in the breeze. Again, the key is redirection. When puppy is looking at something other than you, redirect his attention to you by offering a tidbit or a toy or, if he's really intent on that stick rolling around, use that to entice him. Reward his attention by giving him the treat, toy or object of his interest along with enthusiastic praise. Teach him that good things come from you, not from a distraction. When you take him to his veterinarian, distract him from anything

scary by using a treat or one of his favorite toys. Every time he gets a vaccination, praise him and give him an extra-special treat such as a piece of cheese or freeze-dried liver. Maintain your pup in a steady position for the vet's exam by holding a squeaky toy near his nose. Allow him to chew on the toy to distract from the examination. All these things will teach the puppy that the vet's office is a fun place.

If you are at all dubious or unsure of how to proceed, or if you are experiencing a problem that you don't feel you can handle, contact a professional trainer. You will be happy with the outcome. You'll never understand how you could've lived without such a well-trained puppy that grows into a well-adjusted, properly mannered dog that is a joy to have around.

WORKING WITH A TRAINER

Locating a good trainer is as important as finding the best therapist or medical doctor. A professional trainer will be able to quickly figure out the proper training approach for your pup and apply the training procedures in a positive manner. For example, should puppy have a problem with aggression toward other dogs, the last thing a trainer should advocate is hitting, yelling or dragging the dog around by his neck. Dogs do not understand these behaviors and will become worse when confronted with them. All training should be done in a manner that your dog will quickly understand and enjoy. This is especially important for young pups, as they are easily intimidated and frightened by overbearing mannerisms.

When searching for a trainer, check with dog-owning friends, your vet, a groomer or a local pet-supply store. The best trainers are those to whom people will refer others. Generally, the referral will come from someone who had a good experience with the trainer. There might even be a regular working relationship between the various animal professionals, which is always a positive sign; for example, a trainer who works in conjunction with your vet.

There are three basic ways that trainers operate. The first is by offering a low-cost group class. The group consists of four or more dogs and their owners and is given at a specific place and time for a series of four to ten sessions, depending on the trainer's goals for the class. In this situation, it is difficult for the trainer to address specific behavioral problems, because he must keep the entire group advancing. Should the class have more than ten dogs, the possibility of getting anything out of the sessions will be minimal and your experience may be frustrating. However, there are some very good trainers who offer instruction in a group setting, and you will normally find

them through referral from your veterinarian or a boarding kennel. If you are planning on signing up with a group class through a pet-supply store, request the trainer's credentials. A problem with training your dog in this manner is that the training process is very group-oriented, not allowing the trainer much opportunity to approach each dog and owner as individuals.

Another downside to group training sessions is that a puppy under the age of four months, without all of his vaccinations, cannot attend the class. By the age of four months, your puppy has already learned a lot. If you haven't guided him appropriately up to this point, a group class won't give you all you need to solve the issues your pup presents. However,

A dog with an alert expression—take advantage of his attention and focus it on you.

Dogs can revert to destructive behaviors if not given enough attention, so be sure that your pets get plenty of quality time with their favorite person, you!

it would be a good idea to attend a group class once you've done some individualized training, either on your own or with a trainer who will work with you one-on-one.

The second means of training is to send your dog away for anywhere from two weeks to over a month. This is the most expensive means of accomplishing your goal of a trained dog, and you have very little input in the training process. It works fine as a jump-start if you must be away for a period of time and don't wish for your dog to languish in a kennel. Sending him off for training will give him more stimulation and exercise while you are gone. However, unless you have done extensive research on the trainer and the facility (i.e., visited the facility and watched the training sessions), the chances of your dog's

not being treated the way you would wish are very great. Also, it's not a good idea to send your puppy away during this early and crucial bonding time. It's very important that he remains with you and learns things from you. If you must go away for a while and have no choice, be certain to do your homework. Speak to others who have utilized this service and investigate the area where the dog will be housed. Should he be kept in a large kennel, where many other dogs are also being housed for training, you can bet that he will only receive minimal human attention and socialization. If the trainer accepts only a limited number of dogs, say only up to four, then you can be fairly certain that your dog will receive more attention and socialization, especially if the trainer keeps the dogs

A young Boxer pup, waiting to be molded into a polite and loyal companion. Young pups are like sponges, ready to absorb what you teach them.

in his own house. When the training is complete, you should receive appropriate instruction on how to work with your dog from then on. This can be done in a series of one to four training sessions, depending on the situation.

The third means of training your dog is to partake in individual sessions. This one-on-one situation allows your trainer to address your particular concerns and give you the best advice and help with solving your dog's behavioral problems. Some trainers will even come to your home, giving them the fullest insight into the situation. The training is geared toward the personalities of your pet and yourself. You are taught how to train your puppy and handle difficult situations as they arise. This service will cost a little more than a group class, but less than boarding and training, and you will be getting the most for your money. However, for this to work you must practice with your dog as suggested by your trainer and maintain the training through regular daily training sessions even after your meetings with the trainer have ended.

How can you differentiate between a good trainer and one who is mediocre? First of all, a professional trainer may be a member of a professional trainer's association, such as the International Association of Canine Professionals (www.dogpro.org),

Association of Pet Dog Trainers (www.apdt.com) or National Association of Dog Obedience Instructors (www.nadoi.org). Members of these organizations usually strive to keep up with the latest training methods and tools.

While searching for a trainer, it will also help to ask the right questions. The following are a sampling of questions that will help you find the right trainer:

1. How many years have you been a professional trainer?

"Professional trainer" means that this is the person's prime means of earning a living, not a part-time job. A person who has worked in the field for five or more years is someone who is dedicated to their career and has received appropriate experience in their field. However, someone who has been training for over ten years is even better. The longer the person has been training dogs, the more experience and knowledge they have acquired. However, it can also mean that the person might be using old methods involving force or pain-induced response. Thus the next question.

2. What are your training methods?

A trainer should be able to describe their basic beliefs and methods, and even offer you a chance to preview a training class in progress. There are many ways to train a dog. A professional trainer will not stick to just one method, but will be open to what-

A good trainer gives each dog plenty of one-on-one attention and uses positive methods of training.

ever is necessary to ensure success with your puppy. Every pup is different and therefore every trainer needs to be open to using whatever works, provided it is done humanely and without harming your pup in any manner. A one-method trainer is one who is not experienced enough to work with every problem that might be encountered.

3. *How would this trainer approach the particular problems you are experiencing with your pup?*

Even though the trainer has not met your puppy, he/she should be able to give you some idea of how the training will be implemented.

4. *Does this trainer have experience with destructive or aggressive pups?*

This is very important, for if the trainer uses only one training method, it will not work with all puppies. This trainer may not work with pups that exhibit behavioral problems. If your pup has specific issues, it is best to clarify this before meeting with the trainer.

5. *Is this person willing to teach you how to work with your pup?*

A good trainer spends most of the session teaching you how to communicate with and work with your puppy. Teaching the pup is only a minor part of the service. The puppy is bound to perform well for the trainer. Reality dictates, however, that your pup perform well for you. This person must be proficient at instructing people as well as at teaching dogs.

6. *Will all of your concerns be addressed in this trainer's class?*

Sometimes a group class is not the best approach when dealing with a behavior-modification issue. A group class usually sticks to the basic behaviors. Training on an individual basis will offer more opportunity for the trainer to address all of your concerns, so make certain this is how the trainer approaches this issue unless you are simply searching for basic training knowledge.

7. *Has the trainer published or produced anything pertaining to dog training, such as a book, article or pamphlet?*

A trainer that takes the time to read and write about training is someone who is serious about their work and wishes to provide the best service they can. Handouts and other written material help students learn and offer a means of help when the trainer is not available. Also, it is difficult to take notes while participating in a training class. Having the pertinent information already written is helpful for future reference.

Should you not have access to someone who can offer a positive referral to a trainer, search the Internet and find members of the following professional groups: the International Association of Canine

Professionals (IACP), the Association of Pet Dog Trainers (APDT), the National Association of Dog Obedience Instructors (NADOI), the Society of North American Dog Trainers or the American Dog Trainers Network. All of these organizations' websites offer long lists of trainers, and you can look to find ones in your area. Another great spot to search is K9Trainers.com and the American Kennel Club (AKC) site. Many professional dog trainers wish to prove their methods and abilities through various forms of media, whether through printed material in the forms of books and articles, or electronically on websites. Most search engines will bring up extensive lists of dog trainers.

OUT AND ABOUT

Once your pup is well trained, you can take him anywhere as long as dogs are allowed. Go for long walks through town, romp in the park, hike in the mountains, play on the beach or go to a dog show. If you wish to travel or use your pup as a therapy dog, you will need to earn a Canine Good Citizen® (CGC) certificate. Many hotels and rental establishments will more readily accept the presence of a CGC-certified dog than one that hasn't earned the title. The CGC means that the dog has passed a series of tests that prove that he is friendly and well behaved in public places. If you wish to earn a CGC for your dog, contact a local kennel club

Above all, your trainer must be a true dog-lover.

Your dog will enjoy accompanying you wherever you go, whenever possible. You must provide a safe area for him in the car, such as his crate or a partitioned-off section of the vehicle.

or trainer. They normally have information about test dates and locations.

If you wish to eventually show your pup in obedience, conformation, agility, flyball or other event, again check with the AKC, local breed and kennel clubs and trainers. You can find links to breed and kennel clubs through the AKC's website. You're sure to find one in your area.

Before traveling, be certain to check with your destinations to make sure that they accept dogs. Plan well ahead of time. Know how you and your dog will travel and how your dog will be accommodated upon arrival. There are good books and many websites dedicated to traveling with your pet.

If you are traveling in your vehicle, you will need to either enclose your pup in a comfortable travel crate or fit him with a seat belt. These measures are for his safety as well as your own. You don't want your pup to be injured if you stop suddenly, nor do you want him distracting you while you are driving. If you are on a long trip, be sure to stop every couple of hours so that puppy can stretch his legs and relieve himself. Of course, you will need to bring along plastic bags and/or a "poop scoop" to pick up any droppings. While the car is moving, the pup should have a safe toy to play with, something that is certain to not choke him or distract you.

When traveling by air, you will

need to check with your airline to learn of specific pet policies. There is usually a fee charged for transporting pets. If you have a small dog, he may be allowed in the passenger section, provided that he fits under the seat in his carrier. Otherwise, dogs must travel in the cargo section, which is normally pressurized and temperature-controlled. Many airlines have personnel that check on the animals to assure that they have water and remain in good condition during the trip. They will feed the pets on long trips; some even exercise the pets if the trip is especially long. If your pet is traveling in the cargo area, be sure he is in a hard-sided airline-approved kennel. Put his name, your name, your address and your phone number on the kennel. Also, list any medications, health conditions and behavioral idiosyncrasies that might affect his travel. Make sure you have obtained a health certificate within ten days prior to travel and have plenty of identification attached to him as well as in your wallet. Carry a couple of recent pictures of your dog (as if I even have to mention that one). ID tags are usually enough, but it wouldn't hurt to have your pet microchipped or tattooed as well. Better safe than sorry.

Now that your puppy is an angel and listens in all situations, the sky's the limit. He can accompany you anywhere. He is truly the perfect companion and friend—and all it took was five minutes!

Well-behaved dogs can be used as therapy dogs to bring love, companionship and joy to others.

INDEX

Kennel Club Books®

The pet-book authority, Kennel Club Books
is currently producing the

WORLD'S LARGEST SERIES OF DOG-BREED BOOKS,

including individual titles on 377 different dog breeds, representing every American-Kennel-Club-recognized breed as well as many other rare breeds for which no titles currently exist in English.

Each Kennel Club Breed Book is at least 158 pages, completely illustrated in color, with a hard-bound cover. The prestigious roster of authors includes world authorities in their breeds, as well as famous breeders, veterinarians, artists and trainers.

Explore the world of dogs by visiting kennelclubbooks.com on the Web and find out more about available titles on fascinating pure-bred dogs from around the globe.

Kennel Club Books, LLC
308 Main Street, Allenhurst, NJ 07711 USA
(732) 531-1995 • www.kennelclubbooks.com